The RING THAT CHANGED NOTHING

From Childhood Trauma to Toxic Marriage and Back to Myself

De-De

*To the women out there
who are still struggling.
There is hope and a way out.*

ISBN Paperback: 979-8-9947594-0-0
ISBN Electronic: 979-8-9947594-1-7

Library of Congress Control Number: 2026903394

Portions of this book are works of nonfiction. Certain names and identifying characteristics have been changed.

Printed in the United States of America.

De-De
dedetheauthor.com

Disclaimer

Content Warning:
This memoir contains descriptions of childhood sexual abuse, sexual content, domestic violence, verbal abuse, mental health crises including hospitalization, substance use, explicit language, and emotionally distressing situations. Reader discretion is strongly advised.

Personal Account:
This book recounts the author's personal experiences and perspective. While based on true events, certain names, identifying characteristics, and minor details have been changed to protect privacy. The experiences and opinions expressed are those of the author and do not necessarily reflect those of any other individuals mentioned.

Not Professional Advice:
This book is not intended to provide, and does not constitute, medical, psychological, legal, or professional advice of any kind. The author is sharing her personal journey and recovery process, not prescribing solutions. Readers experiencing abuse, trauma, mental health crises, or related issues should seek guidance from qualified professionals including licensed therapists, counselors, medical doctors, or appropriate authorities.

Educational Purpose:
Information about narcissistic personality disorder, trauma responses, and abuse dynamics is provided for educational awareness based on the author's personal research and experience. This information should not replace professional diagnosis or treatment.

Resources Available:
If you or someone you know is experiencing domestic violence or abuse, please contact the National Domestic Violence Hotline at 1-800-799-7233 or visit thehotline.org. For mental health emergencies, call 988 (Suicide & Crisis Lifeline).

TABLE OF CONTENTS

INTRODUCTION

My complex family background and difficult childhood experiences, including not knowing who my father was until a late age, forced me to deal with strained relationships with my parents and twin sister. My personal challenges, such as past trauma, relationships, and my attempt to join the Army, which ended with a medical discharge, have built my resilience in overcoming adversity and establishing healthy boundaries in my personal life.

My twin sister and I were conceived out of wedlock in 1973 under complicated circumstances. My mother was married to Richard at the time, and while he was serving in Vietnam, she moved in with her blood-related aunt in Connecticut. There, she was seduced by her aunt's husband—her uncle by marriage—and became pregnant with my sister and me. Shortly after Richard returned from Vietnam, my mother gave birth to us. Richard and my mother divorced soon after.

My mother then remarried a man named Gene, and she told us that Gene was our father. We believed this lie throughout our childhood. Everything changed when I was 12 years old. My mother abruptly took my twin sister and me to Richard's house—a man we had never met—and casually announced he was our father. That day shattered everything we thought we knew about our family, but even that "truth" was a lie.

The real truth didn't emerge until I was 19 years old, when I tried to enlist in the Army. After filling out my application, the recruiter pulled me aside and told me the name I'd listed for my father was incorrect. Shocked and confused, I called my mother to demand answers, and all she did was laugh. She found it amusing that I thought I was going to jail for lying on a government document.

I didn't learn who my biological father actually was until about a year and a half ago—decades later. By then, he had already passed away, dying just three months after my mother did. I never met him. My entire childhood felt like a cruel joke, built on layers of lies about something as fundamental as who my father was.

Eventually, I made it to basic training where I loved the structure and camaraderie it offered. Not knowing who my real father was and losing both of my parents within three months of each other has contributed to my trauma in more ways than one. My sister and I were molested by a family friend, with our mother denying the abuse and continuing her relationship with him. We basically grew up in a remote camp with limited supervision, which caused me to develop a constant state of "fight or flight" response due to the trauma.

My first serious relationship was with Steven, which ended traumatically when he broke up with me, even though I was unable to accept it. This experience affected my future relationships, including a four-year relationship with Kip, whom I left because I felt he deserved better than me. Over the years, I have struggled with sexual and verbal abuse, but have learned the importance of setting boundaries, saying "No," and only being around people who respect both and care about my well-being.

I experienced friendship betrayal and financial manipulation. I was excluded from social events and group chats by my friends, despite my financial contribution of $17,000 to a lesbian wedding. Being manipulated into paying for the venue, dress, and other expenses left me excluded from social gatherings. My long-standing friendship with Karen ended when I discovered she was being unfaithful and cheating with my husband, leading me to set boundaries and cut ties with these friends.

This is my personal story of overcoming adversity through resilience, including a tough childhood, a miscarriage, and a difficult situation with my twin sister. My resilience and determination helped me face these challenges without adopting a victim mentality. My journey also taught me about narcissism, gaslighting, and sociopathic behaviors—topics I had never heard of while growing up. Educating myself and staying open to new ideas have helped me heal, and I want to help others experience the same. Recovering from a marriage to a narcissist involves seeking professional help, practicing self-care, learning about narcissistic abuse, rebuilding your support system, and focusing on creating a future vision for yourself.

MY BEGINNINGS

Describing my family background as a child who endured difficult experiences and grew into adulthood is an understatement. Before my twin sister and I were born in Milo, Maine, our arrival was surrounded by a lot of drama with our conception in 1973. My mother was married to my brother's father, and while he was in Vietnam, she moved in with her blood-related aunt in Connecticut. Seduced by her aunt's husband, her uncle, she became pregnant with my sister and me. Shortly after her husband returned from Vietnam, she gave birth to us, and he left her.

My mother remarried another gentleman who had other children, but when we met him, we didn't know that he wasn't our dad. I didn't know that my older sister, my older brother, my twin, and I had different dads. We were told that the man my mother was married to at the time was our father. Nothing was ever said until I was 12 years old, when my mother took my twin sister and me and casually dropped us off at a man's house whom we had never met. He was my brother's father, the man she was married to when she was pregnant with us. We pulled into the driveway, and she tried to pass him off as our father without saying a word.

My mother was a ruthless, heartless woman. I asked her, "Mama, what are we doing?"

"Get out," she yelled.

"But we have never been here before," we said in unison.

"This is where your father lives," she said without any concern for our feelings.

We got out of the car, walked up the sidewalk, and knocked on the front door. When he opened the door, he looked down at us and asked, "What are you doing here?"

"Our mother just said that you are our father," we said together. He let us in, and that day, we met his daughter, whom he had with the woman he married after he left our mother. That whole scene was completely awkward, because now it was evident that he looked at us like trash. In his mind, we were trying to ruin his new marriage.

I didn't know who my dad was until about a year and a half ago, and he died three months after my mother did. My whole childhood has felt like a joke. I have no family on my father's side. On my mother's side, I had one aunt who had one son, and one uncle who was gay—no other aunts or uncles. My family was very small, so I relied more on my siblings than most people do on their cousins or other family members. I wanted my siblings to like me because I didn't have those usual cousin relationships that most families have.

Throughout my life, I have been trying to win over my twin sister's affection. She is very mean to me and is always asking me for favors or things, and I always give them to her because I want her to like me. Even though I have an identical twin sister, many people comment to me that it must have been so fun, but it wasn't. I woke up plenty of times in the morning with her spitting mucus in my mouth. At nine years old, I caught a salamander, and she was jealous, because as little girls, we didn't have anything, so we would look for stuff in the woods. I was flipping over wood and rotten stumps, and I found a salamander. I was so happy. I had it in its little thing overnight, and I couldn't wait to wake up to it the next morning.

When I woke up the next morning, my sister was punching me in the stomach while dropping my salamander into my mouth, and I swallowed it. It was awful. Another time, when I was nineteen, I needed $2 to go to the prom, but she wouldn't give it to me. She had a job, but she couldn't let me have $2 to get tights. She said no. When I would ask her to help me with something, she would say no. I see a pattern here: I do for others, but they do not do for me.

You would think that growing up as young children, we would have bonded a bit because of what we endured, but our mother had us molested. We were all separated at different times, but I didn't know that my twin sister was being molested, too, until I confronted the man who was molesting me. It started when I was in third grade and lasted through my sophomore year of high school.

We would go to school and then head straight out to a shack at the lake, which was more like a large shed with a loft containing four beds. If you have ever seen the movie or read the book, *"Flowers in the Attic,"* that was our life. In V.C. Andrews's *Flowers in the Attic*, the titular flowers symbolize the hidden, repressed, and abused children who are kept locked away in the attic of their wealthy grandmother's mansion, their true potential and growth stunted by neglect and betrayal, much like fragile flowers deprived of sunlight and fresh air. They represent the Dollanganger children's innocence and confinement, a metaphor for their tragic circumstances and eventual transformation into a different kind of "flower" due to the harsh realities of their imprisonment. That was our childhood.

My brother and sister never had sex, but that was the case with us as a set of twins, hidden away in a camp out to the lake, until our mother wanted to use us, because we were cute for men. It is called sex trafficking now. She would bribe us by taking us into town and asking, "Oh, do you want some pizza? Do you want to watch HBO? Do you want to watch a movie?"

But all I wanted was to spend time with my mother, because I never got to see her. She was always out in town, running the roads, and we were left out in the shack at the lake. We literally raised ourselves by watching Oprah, the news, after-school specials, Jerry Seinfeld, and MASH. I didn't know my mother, nor did I know any of her friends. My mother started dating a man who gave her things she'd never had, like nice meals and a little extra money. He wasn't rich, by any means, but she did end up having all four of us molested by him.

My older sister had said that our mother's boyfriend had intimately touched her, so she got kicked out of the house and had to go live with her real father. When my brother, who's one year older than me, was going through some strange things for a young man, like being very angry, sleeping with knives, hammers, and anything sharp. We found them in his bed, and when my mother questioned him, she blamed him.

"Why are you so out of control?" she would yell.

"'Cause your goddamn boyfriend won't stop trying to touch my dick," he yelled back.

That comment got him thrown out of the house, too. My mother told him, "Well, now that you basically turned into a tattletale, you can't come and visit, but you can't live here, so now you have to go stay with your real dad."

That's how we knew my brother had a different dad. My twin sister and I didn't know who our dad was, so we didn't say anything for fear of being thrown out, too. We had no idea what would happen if we told anyone what was going on, and I didn't want to be separated from my twin sister because she was all I had, even though she didn't like me. For years, I had tried to win her affection. After all, I liked her, but it never happened. She asked me if I was gay because I had always wanted to be her friend. I didn't know what that meant and had no idea how to respond to that comment.

One day, I was in the bathroom and started screaming. I completely lost it and fell off the edge of insanity. We were freshmen in high school at the time, and I told her, "He keeps touching me and won't leave me alone."

"He does it to me, too," she confided.

It broke my heart to know he was doing the same thing to her, and that's why I started screaming. She was on the toilet when she told me, and seemed pretty calm about it. We had to stay in control of our emotions at all times; otherwise, we would get in trouble. But feelings of being overwhelmed took over at that moment.

When my mother came into the bathroom to see what I was screaming about, she just yelled, "Deanna, why are you screaming?"

I said, "Mama, cause your boyfriend won't stop touching me. He won't stop touching me. And he does it to my sister, too."

She started slapping me in the face, over a dozen times, while my sister sat on the toilet. I finally stopped crying and asked, "Why am I being slapped in the face?" I was shocked by it and just stood there taking it. "Why don't you hit the other side of my face? This side's numb."

She started hitting the other side of my face. From that point on, we were taken to a house in Brownville Junction that she rented. To this day, I couldn't tell you where it is or if it is still standing, because I must have blocked it out.

During my freshman year, when I was fifteen, the reason my mother and her boyfriend were taken to court was that the school secretary called us into the office.

Immediately, I said to her, "I'm not gonna lie," because she had asked us in the 8th grade, and I had lied because I was scared. "I'm not gonna lie anymore," I repeated. "He… he touches us. He touches me. I felt like I was finally being heard.

My mother then bought a trailer from her boyfriend because he sold used cars and trailers and could offer a good deal. She continued to date him, and we were seen as the troublemakers. She bought the trailer to put my sister and me in and parked it at Ricker's Trailer Park in Milo.

The first time he molested me, I was six years old in the third grade, and it was June. I was in his house, and he was wearing a Santa suit. I kept wondering why Santa was in my room. All I could see was his eyes! I was so scared and begged him to stop saying, "No, please don't! Please!"

Honestly, I don't know what happened after that. He loomed over me in that Santa suit, and I believe I blacked out, something I did quite a bit. I would end up in people's houses in the middle of the night, under their beds. No doubt, I felt the need to go to a safer place. It is also why I have no feeling in my breasts.

So, when the secretary asked us a second time, at least she cared enough to ask us about it again. The whole town knew because our friends weren't allowed to spend the night with us. After all, they knew we were being molested. When we finally went to court, my mother drove us and met her boyfriend there. We had to walk in with him because my mother was still dating him.

He has the nerve to say to us, "How dare you try to ruin my life?"

It was then that I began using very bad language, like fuck, what the fuck? In court, I described what had happened to me and how my mother's boyfriend had built the house with his bedroom, including the door and the window that opened into my room. Since I slept on the bottom bunk, and my sister slept on the top bunk, I could only testify that he would stand there in front of the bunk bed, but I didn't know what he was doing to my sister. I could only testify to what he did to me.

I was overwhelmed and emotional about what was happening, and the people in the courtroom couldn't believe it. My mother wouldn't testify, and then my twin sister lost it when she took the stand. I think my mother's boyfriend had sex with her, to be honest, though I can't say that as a fact because she has never admitted it to me. We've never discussed this before, but she told me he would give her money. He never gave me any money. Not a dime. She had $175 on her one day, and when I asked her about it, she told me that he had given that money to her. It was rare that we would ever have money in our possession. When I saw it, I was happy for her, but when she told me that my mother's boyfriend was giving it to her, I felt scared.

My mother denied everything, claiming we were lying. She ended up staying with him. During the entire time we were molested between the ages of six and seventeen, I feel fortunate that the government didn't come in and take us away or separate us, because I genuinely believe that I would have been raped or molested more times than I was. The whole town knew about it, but no one said a word or did anything to help us.

Somehow, we survived living in that shack down by the lake, and neither one of us said anything, mainly because we were embarrassed and ashamed about what had been happening to us. In my mind, when weird things happen to me, I believe that it is only happening to me, like no one is going to believe me, or how am I going to prove it? It was as if I was living in fight-or-flight mode constantly, but I knew I couldn't be alone with this man. I was in survival mode all the time, and I didn't want to tell my sister what was going on or involve her. I can handle this. When he would start touching me, I would lie still, but he never had intercourse with me.

As I mentioned, it started when I was in third grade, and he would use my little hands to wrap around his penis so he could masturbate while I was sleeping. I would wake up with him ejaculating on me. Then he would fall asleep, and when I would run and tell my mother what just happened, she would get angry with me for waking her up in the middle of the night, and I would get in trouble. When I asked my mother about adding a window to the door, she just said it was for convenience and acted like it was normal.

We told her, "No, it wasn't. He watches us while we get dressed."

When my brother confronted my mother, she took no action. He ended up getting into drugs by the age of twelve as he was being molested by this man from a young age. He has since passed away. My mom didn't help him at all; she literally sold him the pills that he overdosed on.

When I was going through being molested, I mastered a comfortable way to meditate that allowed me to leave my body for the longest time. Being molested, I stopped being able to feel my breasts. Now and then, I hug myself and hold my body, and if anyone is around, they think I am holding my breasts. I can't feel my boobs because I blocked out that sensation of being molested, so when men touch me, I shiver. It almost grosses me out because I'm not prepared to feel any sensation.

As an adult now, I don't have sex for pleasure. I don't believe I ever have. Once or twice, I have, and the man thought it was his doing, but it wasn't - it was my mindset. If I were to have sex, I would need to be alone, where I could enjoy it and feel pleasure. I honestly believe it's because of being molested by my mother's boyfriend, not having a parent in my mother, and not having a daddy, which has caused me anxiety in many ways. I get anxious worrying about everything from being on time for an appointment to wondering if I have enough bologna to make a sandwich. I plan vacations because it's cheaper, and I pay my bills on time, but I don't look ahead; otherwise, I stress myself out.

Living in survival mode, I kept thinking, if I could just get away from this man, I would be fine. When I was in eighth grade, I met a senior who became my boyfriend and helped me deal with what was going on. He and his family knew what was happening and they told me I could spend the night at their home any time I wanted, not to sleep with their son, but just to be safe. They would also include me for dinner and let me hang out, allowing me to show up anytime, no questions asked. It made them feel better knowing I was safe.

That helped me a lot throughout high school, but when their son broke up with me, I felt lost because I didn't have a safe space. It really bothered me, and I didn't know how to handle that situation, especially since we had been together for four years, but I didn't have any say in it when he left me. I also didn't know anything about breaking up with people or relationships, because I'd just been abandoned my whole life by my mother.

When we first met, I was fifteen, and it wasn't as if we jumped into bed right away. We waited an entire year before we kissed, and two years before we had sex. I grew up with him, and now, all of a sudden, he was interested in another young lady. It literally traumatized me. I became one of those girlfriends you probably don't want to dump because every time I saw him talking to someone else, I would come unhinged and scream. It took me a year to get over that relationship, and I soon moved out of town. I will never forget our conversation when he ended our relationship.

He said, "Dee Dee, I'm breaking up with you."

"But I'm not breaking up with you," I replied.

"Well, you don't understand. I'm breaking up with you," he repeated.

And I said, "But you don't understand, I'm not breaking up with you."

It took me a year to accept that we were no longer a couple. After all, I knew he loved me, and we spent every weekend together going to the mall, swimming, the movies, and hanging out by the lake during the late 80s and early 90s. He was what I didn't have growing up, and then he just decided he was done. I didn't know how to take that, so I had to learn how to be done. I didn't date or pursue other men, maybe just some casual meetings during the summer, but nothing serious, and then I would get bored with them.

2

MEETING CHRISTOPHER

I met a gentleman in the fall after just turning twenty-one, who was quite handsome and meant everything to me. His mother was a kindergarten teacher, and his father was an 8th-grade teacher. He looked Italian, but he was Canadian—polite and perfect for me. When I first met him at a party, he was engaged, but he caught my eye. I couldn't take my eyes off him. We didn't speak, so I enjoyed the party. A year went by, and then I ran into him again at another party where I had been drinking. After being molested for so many years, I like to be in control and have no problem approaching any man I am interested in.

So, I was aggressive and said to him, "Hey, I like you. I saw you about a year and a half ago, and I really like you. Let's start dating."

"No, I'm engaged," he replied.

"I don't care. I waited a whole year and a half to see you again. If you're not married now, I don't care. This is my chance," I said to him with a smile.

Overhearing our conversation, his brother intervened and said, "He's engaged."

"I'm not taking no for an answer," I replied. "I'm gonna wait here until the engagement's over."

They assumed I was drunk and laughed it off. My dating skills (or lack thereof) date back to when I was with my first boyfriend, when he dumped me. I started stalking him, following him to college. He went to the University of Maine in Orono. I figured out where his classes were, and since it was before computers and social media, I had to dig and check license plate numbers. I had to go to where I thought one of his friends' friends worked, connecting the dots. My friends call me 'Harriet the Spy.'

Eventually, I found out where Christopher lived, and his roommate caught me hiding behind the garage.

"What are you doing here?" he asked, his voice filled with surprise.

Christopher walked out, and I said to him, "I really, really like you, and I want to hang out with you."

My hard work paid off. By the time I was twenty-three, we were dating and planning to move in together. It was a lot of fun for another three years. Smart as a whip, he taught me a new word every week because I was not well educated. He was so patient, kind, and loving, but I left him because I thought he deserved better. He deserved to be with someone who could light up his life, not a goofball like me, whom he had to be worried about all the time.

Even though I had already met Christopher, when I went back to Milo, I hid because I didn't want to be the one who shot her fucking head off. So, I moved to Bangor and started working at the Bangor Daily as a telemarketer. However, I speak loudly, even when I'm on the phone. I would yell, "Hello, this is so-and-so from Bangor Daily, would you like a subscription to the Bangor Daily?"

The telemarketers next to me complained that I was too loud and couldn't hear the people on their calls, so they moved me to my own room, which felt like my own office. I was excited, but it turned out I was still too loud, and they had to move me to another floor—the top floor—because I was being so noisy. Since I was placed so far away from everyone and no one could hear me, I started calling all my girlfriends, especially Christopher, who eventually became my boyfriend at the time, because I didn't have a phone at home.

One of the people I called was my gay uncle, my mother's brother. I was, what you'd say, his favorite, and could ask him for anything, so I asked for $500 a week, and he was kind enough to give it to me. He was the CEO of a big shoe chain in Puerto Rico and did quite well until it closed. He has passed away now, but back when I was in my early 20s and growing up, I think he knew what I was going through, but I didn't tell him. He would come and check on us at least once a month and bring us clean clothes when we were younger. When I got older and got my driver's license, I discovered where my uncle lived and would visit him. One thing I noticed as I grew older was that I never had company. I was always the one going to see people. No one ever came to see me.

When I was with Christopher, God loved him, I ended up leaving him because I really felt that he deserved better. Because he did. In my heart of hearts, he was too good for me, like when he would teach me a word every day. I didn't give myself enough credit, coming from nothing and eating out of dumpsters, to think that I deserve to be with someone like him. After being with him for four years, I finally realized how amazing and beautiful he was, and how much more he could give to someone else who probably deserved it more than I did.

He ended up marrying a woman who resembled me and had two children. When I left Christopher, I met a guy who worked at Sears. I didn't know about pill heads and stuff, like people taking prescription pills for recreational reasons. Well, he did, but I wasn't aware of that—I was a bit naïve. He was so good-looking, and he got me pregnant, but I had a miscarriage. I was carrying around a dead fetus in my body and didn't know it.

I could smell it on my skin and started asking everyone, "Smell me, do I smell death to you? Why do I smell death?"

The typical response to me was, "Shut up, De-De, you're just crazy."

I said, "No, no, no, I stink. I'm just in a haze. I smell death."

That summer, I went out to visit my twin sister and became very sick. At first, I thought it was because I was in Tennessee with atopic dermatitis and dealing with the heat of the summer.

When my sister asked me if I was okay, I said, "Oh, this is my atopic, I'm getting sick, I gotta go back."

When I returned home, I went to the doctor and told her, "I'm so sick, and I smell like death! What's happened to me?"

She said, "You're carrying a dead fetus that is 3 months old, but it's been dead. You've been carrying around a 3-month-old fetus."

Shocked, I asked, "For how long?"

"Two months," she replied.

"Well, can you get it out of me?" I asked, ready to get this over with.

"No, you're going to have to pass it," she replied.

"What do you mean? Like, a cat does when it has to abort the litter?"

"Basically," she said.

So, I called Christopher up, even though we weren't dating. I didn't tell him what was going on; I just told him I needed him. He drove three hours to come and pick me up.

When he arrived, he said, "I'm going out to the lake where I grew up with the guys I knew. But please, it's not about you. I want to have fun. Don't be, like, kissy-kissy, or think that we're gonna get back together."

I said, "No, no, no, I want help. Can I just be near you?

Again, I was looking for some support, some safe place I could be because I was carrying a dead child. I needed a safe place, and Christopher was always a safe place. So, he took me out with him to Schoodic Lake. We were there with all the guys that we both knew and went to school and college with.

Later in the evening, around 9 p.m., I began to feel very cold. Mind you, this was summer, so it didn't make sense, but I was freezing. They didn't have any indoor plumbing, and I remember going outside, where they were by the water, and they were looking at me.

They asked, "De-De, are you alright?"

I didn't say anything, and went to the outhouse, and gave birth by myself to a dead baby, and it hurt so bad, I almost passed out from the pain. I could hear it plop out into the water. I had no idea what a three-month-old fetus would look like, but when I took the flashlight to look at it, it looked like just a blob. Somehow, I felt relieved and was glad it didn't have a face. I knew I was going to be all right, so I went back inside, but now I was getting so hot, hot, hot.

I had no idea what was happening to me, but I didn't want to bother Christopher, especially since he told me not to be a problem, taking me out to the lake. What was I going to do? The place had bunk beds, so I climbed up to the top bunk and just lay there hemorrhaging for 11 hours until the next morning. One of my friends who slept on the bottom bunk was covered in my blood that dripped through my bunk bed and was dripping onto his sleeping bag. He yelled at me because I ruined his LLB sleeping bag!

I said, "I just gave birth to a dead baby outside in the outhouse."

"What?" he asked.

"What did you say?" Christopher asked who had just come in and heard what I said.

"I didn't want to ruin anyone's day. We were all just hanging out," I replied.

Immediately, Christopher took me to the nearest emergency room and the doctor questioned me as to what had happened.

When I told him I had been bleeding for eleven hours, he said, "What? You were hemorrhaging for eleven hours? You are lucky to be alive."

Thankfully, I was fine and just had to wear pads. I stayed with him for two days, then returned to my apartment. However, when I got yelled at by the guy for ruining his LLB sleeping bag, that really upset me, like that was all he could think about; instead of saying something like, "Good job for surviving. Glad you didn't die last night." I never get a pat on the back. Instead, I have learned to give myself a pat on the back because I know where I came from, where I am, and where I'm going.

That said, it wasn't until I joined the Army that I realized our mother had lied to us for years about who our father was. After filling out my application, the recruiter came to me and said, "The name of your mother is correct, but the name of your father is not."

"What?" I asked, confused and shocked by his statement.

"The name of your father is incorrect," he repeated.

Immediately, I called my mother to ask her who our father was, and all she could do was laugh. My mind was racing as I thought I was going to jail for lying about my dad on a government document, while my mom just laughed over the phone. When I went into the Army, I got the shit kicked out of me because I came from Milo, Maine, and was now in Fort Jackson, South Carolina. It is the first town in New England and in the United States to have a KKK march during daylight hours, and my great-great-grandfather led that march. I'm not racist, though I was taught that I was the elite and superior race.

When I got on a bus filled with black women, I was one of four white women there. I literally stood at the front of the entire bus and said, "You must all be so excited that we white girls are here." That was when they kicked the shit out of me. At the time, I had no idea why they were beating me up. I got off that bus, and the minute I got a chance, I called my mother.

When she answered the phone, I yelled, "Mama!"

"Oh my God, Deanna, what have you done now?" she asked, sounding annoyed.

"Mama, black people don't like us," I said emphatically. "I just got the shit kicked out of me," and all she did was laugh. She never said anything that made sense and laughed. I quickly learned (the hard way) that there is no superior race.

I managed to make it through basic training, but they kicked me out four days before graduation. Back then, I was strong physically, mentally, and much more emotionally, but I have atopic dermatitis that pops up when I get hot and sweaty. When it started happening, I could jump into the lake and cool off to prevent it from getting out of control quickly. I was always clean, even though we were dirt poor, but since we lived on a lake, we were always clean, whether we were lugging water, boiling water, swimming in the water, brushing our teeth, shaving our legs in it, we were always in water.

But when I went to the Army at Fort Jackson, South Carolina, wearing full military gear, out in the sun, I would sweat profusely. However, there was no place to go to wash if my dermatitis acted up. Wearing all that clothing and military gear for ten hours, anything attached to me, around my waist, between my legs, my knees, my feet, my ankles, got this disgusting, thick, blistery rash. And it itched. I put up with it for three months and never told a soul because I didn't want to go back to Milo. Three people from Milo went to the military, were kicked out and when they came back home, blew their head off. That was NOT going to be me.

I will put up with this rash, and since being molested for so many years, I couldn't feel my skin anyway. It would show up in the middle of the night, and I would talk myself into calming down, get some ice packs to put on me without anyone seeing what I was doing.

One day, we had a drill out in the desert, a sandy area of South Carolina, where it was so hot, and the blisters were all over me. I couldn't take it anymore and started taking my clothes off, including all my gear.

My drill sergeant yelled, "Private Sartell, what are you doing? Have you lost your Goddam mind?"

I said, "I can't take it. No more drills, I can't take it," as I stood there with my underwear and bra on, turning all the way around for them to see my body."

"Holy fuck!" everyone around me exclaimed with their eyes wide open.

My whole body was covered in that rash, so I received a medical discharge for atopic dermatitis. That is also why I take many showers, especially when I get sweaty. However, I loved being in the Army, particularly the security, camaraderie, and discipline that basic training provided. I cried when they kicked me out.

3

ADULT ENTERTAINMENT

After surviving the miscarriage at age twenty-seven, the next day, he and I drove to his house in Rangeley. While driving, he looked at me and said, "You know, De-De, I like you, you're my friend, but you can't live here because you drive me crazy." We were complete opposites: I like to talk with a lot of energy, and he is a hard worker and very focused. I knew I was a bit too much for him, but he still loved me and said, "Let's think about something that you can do."

"You know what? What if I were a stripper?" I asked, waiting for his response. Even though I did not have boobies then, I had nice nipples. At least, that is what I have been told. "It's a lot about personality. You know, would you be mad at me or disown me if I became a stripper?"

"No. I wouldn't. You could do it," he replied.

"Alright," I said, thinking about my next step. So, I called my mother and said, "Mama. Christopher said that it'd be alright if I were a stripper. What do you think? You think I could do it?"

"Yes, Deanna, you've got that personality," she replied.

I said, 'Alright, I'm going to call my sister and see if she approves of it," I said. And her response was, "Go ahead. You got this."

As I am writing this, I started to cry because my twin sister calls me a whore now, knowing that I was a stripper. I called her for her validation, her acceptance, and now she calls me a whore, though that was thirty years ago. What people need to understand about the adult entertainment industry is that it is, simply, a business. I looked at it as a job and nothing more; there was nothing romantic about it. So many people think we walk around being horny all the time and ready and willing to be on our backs at any given moment for sex, but we don't. We clock in like anyone else going to a job. Plus, we have to prepare for the shows on our list that we must perform that day.

I didn't have an education. I still don't, even though I attended high school at Penquis Valley, where they selected students likely to receive a better education. For example, my second cousin took college-prep courses and was not considered dirt-poor white trash. This was not the case for me, nor for many other kids. We were offered classes like Home Economics, Sewing, and other no-brainer classes. In other words, I don't have a learning process because I wasn't taught to process anything.

For example, everything was given to me like a simple, plain white paper plate. I didn't know that I was to put things on my plate as I learned. Growing up, my plate was always empty, but now I know how to fill it, and I am proud of that because I am doing it on my own. I don't get recognition for anything. A pat on the back, so foreign to me, but I'm all about personality. I have to be a comedian, an entertainer, and someone who makes people laugh. I'm tiny, built, and cute.

When I was being molested, and watching my mother struggle with her weight, men only liked her when she was more secure with her body and slim. I learned that at a young age, I had to be petite, and men always found me attractive. And that's all I knew. It may be a cliché, but stripping was my only way of making money at the time. I didn't know any other way. I just knew I had to find a way to make an income.

However, it ended up being a lot of fun. All I did was call the local strip club and didn't even interview face-to-face. I said, "Hi. My name is De-De."

The man who answered the phone asked, "Well, what do you look like?"

"Well, I'm 20…" I fibbed. I was 27, but I looked 18.

He said, "Okay, come on in."

When I arrived at the strip club, I was wearing a little T-shirt with an image of the Taco Bell dog from the 90s, and though I didn't have any boobs to speak of, the woman who interviewed me said, "You're so cute."

I was the only one there who had 6-pack abs, though I didn't realize how important that was at the time. I literally didn't even know what abs were. I asked someone, "How come your stomach doesn't look like mine? Is this normal?"

"Those are muscles," said another dancer named Chantelle. "You look great."

I said, "No way!"

"Yeah, you look great, De-De."

My stage name was Jade, but the first dance I performed was so lame because I didn't know any moves. The only music I knew was music from other TV strip shows, like Striptease with Demi Moore. So, I had to come up with ideas in my head with specific ways to move, but I immediately found out that I wasn't considered a sexy woman. My body looks sexy, but my personality isn't sexy. I'm goofy and funny! I would get stuck upside down trying to do a move, but instead of getting mad, I would laugh and fall. Men would throw money at me and say, "Oh my God, she's so cute, she's so funny, she's so ridiculous."

However, I also did private shows because I knew where the money was. You had to be at least eighteen to strip, but you had to be at least twenty-one to do private shows, because occasionally they want you to have a cocktail with them. When my boss thought I was 18, because I looked so young, I said, "No, no, no, I'm 27. I'm the same age as Jordan. I want to do private shows."

She said, "Okay," but I soon discovered that performing private shows required more than just dancing. Not to make light of it, but it was not uncommon for me to give a stranger a hand job; however,

I was considered a professional, and I was getting paid for doing so. That was my mindset. I was providing a service, and men were willing to pay top dollar for my services. I was making a lot of money doing what my slutty friends were doing at the bar for free. And I didn't understand that mindset because they were struggling financially in their own personal lives, and I wasn't. I filed taxes every year for two and a half years under the Adult Entertainment category.

I ended up with four sugar daddies who loved me. The college guys in their twenties weren't attracted to me because all they wanted were the women with big boobs, but it was their fathers, uncles, and older men who were drawn to me. I was paid to call them Uncle Bill, sit on their lap, bounce, and be cute. I was paid to wear little dresses and pee on men for $5,000. All I had to do was drink water for 45 minutes, wear a little dress, and stand over a guy. I wouldn't even let the guy touch my ankles, because then I couldn't focus on what I was doing. I'll admit that the men I peed on were gross, but I was one of the ones who provided services for them. A couple of them wanted to sleep with me, but they were in their seventies and too old for me. When I would play with their penis, it was like fondling jelly and never got firm.

Generally, you would not realize I was an adult entertainer if you saw me on the street, unless you hired me, because I didn't dress like one. When it came to buying dresses, I never had to shop at the boutiques where regular adult entertainers shop for their thongs or boots. I shopped at regular clothing stores and bought kids' clothes because they fit me, and that is generally what the men who paid me wanted to see me in.

During my time as an adult entertainer, I was the highest-paid stripper just by selling the underwear that I wore that day for a pantie company online. I got $250 a pair, with a vagina wipe, but if I wore them all day, the price would go up considerably, depending on what I did while wearing them. For example, if I worked out in them and sweat more between my legs, my panties would be worth top dollar. If I sat around in a pair all day, I would get $500 to $1,000.

However, I was intimate with two of the other older sugar daddies, and although they were married, I didn't concern myself with their personal lives. Again, this was work. I clocked in and out and was very professional. I never dressed slutty or showed up at someone's house in fishnet stockings, but it was the most fun job I've ever had.

As a professional at the club, I had to choose three songs that were part of the rotation for the dancers when we were on stage. Remember, I wasn't sexy, I was cute and fit. When it was time to take off our clothes, I would trip and fall, so instead, I would be paid $100 to do one-handed pull-ups naked from these bars that hung from the ceiling. That was $100 for each pull-up I performed, and all I can say is thank God for weird men who would pay me to do this.

My stripping career on stage lasted about a year, after which I spent another year performing at bachelor parties and personal shows, as that was where I could earn the most money, around $15,000 to $20,000 a week. As you read this, you may wonder why I would leave the industry, but the truth is that there were several reasons. Through it all, I started using cocaine, something I had never done before. It is the only thing I've ever done in my life, willingly, that I feel guilty about.

Cocaine made me feel so remorseful. I wasn't a cocaine slut, but I hated the habit. I would never do it at work because 'coke' was weird for me. When I did coke, I wanted to be alone. I couldn't dance. I couldn't hear music. I couldn't even talk. Picture me not talking! I didn't want anyone around me, but I craved the taste of it. The minute it went up my nose, I could taste it in the back of my throat. It actually tastes like weed killer. There's an Orkin weed killer that we have to apply to our lawn every year, and ever since I started using 'coke,' when I open that weed bag and smell it, I'm reminded of how it tastes in the back of my throat. It's called the 'drip.' I was addicted to the drip, and it tastes so good that I craved it, and I never craved anything.

What I didn't realize is that I have an addictive personality. The experts tell me it is because of being molested starting at a young age. For example, I would steal a bottle of NyQuil from the Hillside Market grocery store every night to drink before going to bed, so that I could sleep. My mother didn't know about it until my twin sister tattled on me.

She said, "Mama, De-De's addicted to NyQuil. She drinks it every night."

All I could think was that it was because I was being molested every night. I didn't say that, but that's what I was thinking.

Then, my mother would say to me, "You're a loser, you're disgusting, you're stealing," but I couldn't explain to her why I was doing it, because no matter what, it was going to be my fault. So, I had to hide the NyQuil somewhere else. All I can say is that I survived my childhood. However, I have since learned that traumatic events in one's life can alter brain development and our stress response systems, leading to issues later in life, such as relationship problems, managing emotions, and navigating daily life. My journey continued with the birth of my son.

4

MY SON

I became pregnant with my son when I was twenty-eight, while I was still seeing his father. When I found out I was pregnant, I told him, "I don't want to have a baby with someone who doesn't want to have a baby. So, do you want to have a baby? Having this talk is vital to me, so do you really want to have a baby?"

"Yeah, let's do this," he replied.

And then he cheated on me and left me, but that being said.

I was booked for a private show that night, and though I considered myself an adult entertainer, when I was two weeks pregnant, I knew that I was going to have to get naked and probably have to perform something sexual. It made me feel terrible knowing that I was carrying my child. I was so ashamed. I couldn't do it. Despite all that I had been through, I maintained my standards, self-worth, and boundaries. I was in that hotel room and quickly excused myself, stepping outside.

I sat down on the steps outside the hotel, put my hand over my stomach, and said to my baby, "You know what? I'm not going to do this anymore. Mommy's going to make a better life for you, and we're going to do a lot better."

After that, I told my male gay friend, who put me in touch with his sister, who works for the Department of Human Services (DHS).

She managed to set me up to receive everything the state of Maine has to offer for single mothers with babies. I love hanging out with gay men because they never try to sleep with you or touch you while you're sleeping. Anyway, that meant getting checks from TANF (welfare checks and food stamps), coupons from Sears, laundry soap, and even getting mechanical service for my car.

While I was pregnant, his father had lied to me and no longer wanted to be in the picture. He didn't feed me, and he was nowhere to be found. I went to his boss's house one night and said, "Geez, I haven't seen my baby's daddy in a week or two. Do you know where he is?"

"He is building houses about four or five hours away," he replied. "He's at the job site."

"Usually he calls, but I haven't seen him. And I'm hungry. Not ashamed to tell you if I'm hungry," I said. "I'm hoping you'll offer me a sandwich or something. Maybe you could get him to give me some money."

He said, "He's been staying with that ex-stripper, and he is living with her in Lewiston."

She is a woman whom I used to work with at the strip club, so to hear that he was living with her and her son really upset me. I called my friend, Billie, who was admitted to the Maine Mental Health Institute, and found that she had escaped and soon came to my apartment to drive with me to Lewiston to tear her apart. We drove to her place, which was four hours away, and my baby's daddy was surprised to see me there.

"What are you doing here? This is none of your business," he said, wanting to get rid of me.

"Really? You're my son's father, and you're living here with her," I replied.

Billie scared him because he knew she was mentally ill, and that's when he realized and said, "You can't just come here whenever you want. I'm not going just to let this happen."

I took control of the situation with my baby, found an apartment, and handled things, but I didn't do it alone. I called up one of my sugar daddies, whom I met in Bangor. It was nice of him to meet me at the hospital, as he had a doctor's appointment. We met in the cafeteria of the Eastern Maine Medical Center when I was pregnant. No one could tell I was pregnant, wearing a winter coat, because I'm so petite.

When I saw him, he said, "De-De, it's so nice to see you, I haven't seen you in… oh."

I said, "9 months?"

"Yeah," he replied. "Why?"

I took my jacket off, and said, "Well, because I'm pregnant."

Immediately, he said, "It's not mine! Is it?"

"No, no, no, don't be silly. No, it's not yours," I said, reassuring him. And then we laughed about that, and I said, "Listen, I need to move, and I need 30 grand to hire a mover, get my stuff out of storage, and pay my old apartment rent. Can you help me move?"

"Okay, he replied, "When do you need it?"

"As soon as possible," I said. I needed to hire a mover, retrieve my belongings from storage, and settle my outstanding apartment rent. I came up with that number, and he gave it to me. He helped me move to Lewiston, three hours away from Bangor. You may recall all the dating I did, and how I used to stalk the men I was interested in or dating. I moved around the corner from where my son's father and his new girlfriend lived.

One day, when I was out walking my son, he was out walking her son, with her, and she was wearing my clothes. I couldn't believe it.

I walked right up to her and said, "You're wearing my clothes." Then I looked at him and asked, "Why did she get my clothes?"

I almost beat the shit out of her, but my son's father said, "I gave them to her. You looked so cute in those pants that I wanted her to have them."

I swear to God, when I saw her in my Tommy Hilfiger pants, I was losing my mind. I bought them at T.J. Maxx, and they looked great on me, but when I went to wear them, they were missing. I couldn't believe it. That was bullshit. After my son was born, his father tried to rebuild a relationship with me, but that is when I found out he was doing crack. I didn't know this until the second time he was arrested, and by then, I had already had my baby.

I allowed my son to visit his father. What mother doesn't try at least once in a toxic relationship to enable that bond between the father and child? So, I took my son over to his father's place and left him there for a few hours to play on the Xbox. He was only two at the time.

So, I left my son with his father, thinking they would play on the Xbox. When I went to pick up my son, he handed me a tiny Ziploc baggie and said, "Mama, Mama," waving it at me. It was a bag that contained crack. That's the last time he saw his father. After that incident, he set my apartment's front door on fire and broke the Xbox. Since he had built houses and was in good shape, he climbed up the back of my four-story apartment building and ended up on my back deck.

I lived on the top floor of the building and thought I was safe that high up, so you can imagine how scary it was to see him throwing a fit and yelling in my face. We've had altercations before where he would hit me, and I would hit him back. In fact, I've been arrested twice already. I have been in jail defending myself because of him physically hitting me. He bit me in the nose, punched me in the face, and broke my ribs. Growing up in the type of household that I did, raising myself, I fought back, which unfortunately, got me arrested.

Now that I'm a mother, this time I just put my hands in my pockets. He had me arrested the second day my son came home from the hospital. It happened when he came around the corner to my apartment after he got in a fight with his girlfriend, whom he beat up.

He said, "I want to see my son."

I said, "Well, he's sleeping. He's in the bassinet. He's sleeping."

He got so angry that he grabbed my refrigerator with both hands and knocked it over, sending all its contents flying to the floor. As a mother of a two-day-old baby on welfare, seeing all my groceries all over the place was horrendous. Back in the day, we didn't have cell phones, so he called his mother on my house phone, and because I ran my mouth, I said, "Yeah, who are you talking to? Your mother? The only dumb bitch that will believe you?" That is when he slapped me.

By this time, the neighbors in the apartment beside us could see in the window, and he was yelling to them, "Help! She's hurting me! She's hitting me! She dumped the refrigerator."

He fucking turned it all on me, and when the police showed up, I was arrested. I couldn't believe it. I said, "Well, what about my baby? Who's going to take care of my baby?" And because I said that, my son's father bailed me out the next morning under his brother's name. He said, "It just hurt me so bad hearing you care so much for my son."

"Your son?" I yelled. "That's my son. You just had me arrested for fucking nothing."

I'll take a beating before I put my hands up, but I will not let anyone talk badly to my son. My son is my son. I would take a bullet for him. Everyone who knows me knows that you treat my son with the utmost respect, or you're going to hear from me. My son is a saint with Asperger's syndrome. He doesn't even know how to lie, he's just polite and friendly and he is mine.

Asperger syndrome or Asperger's is a term sometimes used to describe a developmental disorder that's part of the autism spectrum disorder (ASD). However, it's a controversial term that no longer exists as a medical diagnosis, so fewer people use it to describe their condition. People with this type of ASD often struggle with social interactions. They may follow a specific routine and have a limited range of interests. Doctors sometimes call Asperger's a "high-functioning" form of ASD, meaning its symptoms are generally less severe than other types of autism spectrum disorder. However, the term "high-functioning" is also debated. Many autistic individuals prefer to use terms like "low support needs" and "high support needs" to describe their position on the spectrum.

Knowing that my son had this form of autism, I didn't want to put a spotlight on him or me by dressing provocatively or flirtatiously in any way as a mother. Being a mother for 18 years to my son, I never showed cleavage, because as a stripper, I didn't want that persona following me into motherhood. That was a job, a different career, and another chapter of my life. Now I'm a mother.

Even though I paid for breast implants myself, I don't wear shirts that show my cleavage. Most strippers had theirs paid for by their own sugar daddies, but mine preferred me with small breasts. As I raise my son and become a mother, my physique, body, and personality have not changed. I looked like a very young lady, which could easily be mistaken for a stripper. I thought if I showed any cleavage, I would be mistaken for a stripper with my new breasts. I wear dresses and look like I'm going to the PTA.

In fact, I've never been to the beach with my son in a bikini, because I don't want people to think I'm still a stripper, though I am built the same way. I still struggle with people still thinking that I am still in the adult entertainment industry, but now I am in my fifties. As an older woman, I have noticed that my body has not changed, and I refer to myself as an adult child.

Raising my son and being a mother mean a great deal to me, and I am always aware that my behavior and appearance could affect how he is treated. The way your child acts reflects you as a mother, and I am a good mother. No one can say otherwise!

When my son was in the third grade, one of the teachers came up to me and said, "You're doing a great job!"

"What do you mean?" I asked, my face showing surprise.

"Your son is so good and helpful," she replied.

"Well, he is doing a great job," I said.

"No. You are doing a great job," she said, insisting that I realize that I was being a great mother.

"No one has ever said that to me before," I replied. I literally pat myself on the back because no one else does, but she did. That secretary at the elementary school was so nice that I brought her chocolates.

Stripping was fun, but I love being a mom. From being molested and treated like a bag of shit, one of the things I liked about being a stripper was that I was in charge of myself and my body. I was the one who got to say, "No, you can't touch me," or "Get your hands off me." I set the limits. I finally took charge of my own body and what was going to happen to it. I loved it. Plus, I was getting paid.

It might sound crazy, but the men who paid to hang out with me treated me with more respect and kindness than most of the men I've dated. It seemed like they chose to spend their extra social time with me, not because I was getting paid but because they genuinely wanted to be with me. They listened to my opinions, were friendlier, and showed me respect—something I had not experienced before. Without sounding weird, they made me feel like I was human, not just some piece of trash.

Having been molested, I felt like I was destined to be one of those after-school special kids—always sad, ignored by others, and eventually turning to drugs. During high school, I was suicidal and attempted to take my own life twice, though I wasn't fully aware of it at the time. When I would experience anxiety, it would get so intense that I would blackout because I had no idea how to deal with it. My subconscious took over, and without realizing it, I kept slicing my arm or wrist, but since I only used the dull side of the knife, nothing happened.

However, one time, at the age of seventeen, I was in downtown Milo and used a piece of broken glass to cut myself. My sister was driving by and noticed me there in a fearful state. Immediately, she stopped and yelled at me from her car, calling me stupid, ignorant, and dumb. I just wanted a hug! She left me standing there with a bleeding arm. I walked home, which was probably ten miles, washed my arm, and wrapped it with a white towel. All I could do was hold on to it tight while I lay in my bed.

5

MEETING MY FUTURE HUSBAND

Two years after I had my son, I met my future husband while working as an adult entertainer. Since I was not very educated, I tried to attend college. The state of Maine helped me gain admission to the Community College of Central Maine in Lewiston, but I was utterly lost and quit. This was when computers and laptops began gaining popularity. In high school, I didn't learn anything about computers. To this day, I still don't know anything about computers, so I have to have my nephew help me. No one has ever taught me anything. I'm basically self-taught my whole life. When people put something in front of me and leave me alone with it, I think to myself, "What am I supposed to do with this?"

For example, the first time I went to dinner with my husband while we were dating, he took me to a fancy restaurant. He knew I wasn't familiar with the menu because I had never been to this type of restaurant before. He could have easily ordered for me after we discussed the menu together without the waiter being present. He knew I struggled with reading, so I just assumed that if I told him what I wanted to eat, he would tell the waiter. When the waiter came and asked what I would like for dinner, I just looked at my boyfriend, who looked at me with a confused expression. I wanted him to give the waiter my order. When I tried to pronounce the entrée I wanted, he just laughed at me. I knew then that even though I wasn't alone, I was on my own.

That being said, eventually I returned to adult entertainment as a mother. The only way I could justify doing this was by putting my son in a pre-preschool that the state of Maine offered for welfare mothers. The children were being watched and educated simultaneously. He was two years old when I started that program. While he was in preschool, I did try dancing during the day because I didn't want him to be without me in the evenings. But because the money was barely there during the day at the club, I looked for another job doing private parties so I could make a living for myself and my son.

I made a phone call to a woman from Companions in Portland, who offered bachelor parties and private events in adult entertainment. When I went for the interview, it was easy because all they wanted to do was look at me to ensure I was what they were looking for.

She said, "Oh my God. You are so cute and look so young."

I was hired immediately and began performing in shows, a role I held for about a year. While I was doing that, I hung out with the owner, as her son was the same age as my son, so we had playdates all the time. Then, I would get to work, and she would receive calls for a girl to go to work. Without me even realizing it, I was getting all the jobs because I happened to be right there with my son, having a playdate.

The owner would say to me, "Go ahead. Go do the show. It is only for an hour straight down the road. I'll watch them while they're playing, you're fine." I was so grateful knowing that my son was safe, playing with her son, and making money. However, I didn't realize that she wasn't a good babysitter, but I'll get back to that shortly.

While working for her, a man called her a few times after seeing my photo on the website and requested a private show from me. At that point, websites for adult entertainment were already online. Before that, anyone booking a girl for a show or bachelor party had no idea who would show up. Now, you can see what the girl looks like on the website. However, she didn't send me and instead kept sending her other friend, Tatiana, who needed extra work.

He said to her, "No, this isn't the girl who is on the website. I want the girl who's on the website."

So, she called me again, but I was already at another show at a hotel with a doctor from New York, who was smoking crack. He literally had his crack in tinfoil sitting on the light bulb in the lamp to heat it so he could smoke it.

I called her and said, "This motherfucker's smoking crack. I am going to get high with all this smoke in the room."

Immediately, she said, "Get out. Leave now."

"Really?" I asked, worried that it would anger the client.

"Don't worry about it, I'll call him and take care of it. Tell him you have to go, and you have another show right now, that I just booked."

"Okay," I replied, grateful to leave that hotel room.

"I just booked you for a private show with another man who has been requesting you. He keeps calling and really wants to see you. He's just down the highway at the next exit," she replied, giving me the name of the hotel. She had never mentioned this guy to me before, probably because she was sending another girl who she felt needed the money more.

"Sweet," I said. "I'm on it."

When I went to meet him, he opened the door wearing only a towel. He said he was forty-two, but I found out later he was forty-seven. He was Italian with dark hair and was very attractive.

I said to him, "Damn. I have to tell you, my flavor of the month is Italian." I love Italian men and literally dated five of them.

He was a little weird at first, acting like this was the first time he had ever done something like this. Though I didn't know what to expect, I had heard all this before, and I knew it was bullshit because he had already called three times and seen my friend twice. I knew he was lying to me (red flag), and I have always said, if you are going to lie, why bother even speaking? Save yourself from a lie.

Anyway, he started showing me pictures of his wife and kids in a Ferrari, traveling in Paris and Africa, and all I could think was how lame this was. I was really bored. Finally, I asked, "Well, do you want a show or not?"

He said, "Yeah, I just don't know what to expect," acting very innocent.

When he took his towel off, he was completely naked, so I gave him a blowjob. I had a bra and undies on, so I took my bra off, thinking that maybe, while I was, you know, giving him a blowjob, that he might want to fondle my breasts or something for him to play with. He didn't. He literally just put his hands behind his head with his elbows wide open. It reminded me of the movies I have seen when men sit back and look like they are getting the best blow job ever. Maybe he was enjoying it, but he didn't try to touch me at all.

Afterward, he said, "Wow, that's never happened to me before." I knew it was bullshit. If you're in the business long enough, you know it's bullshit.

So, I said, "Oh, really?" but he tipped me only $160, which is a remarkably low tip. On my way out, he asked if he could call me again, but since I didn't know him like my regulars, I said, "Listen, if you ever want to see me again, just call the office.

He said, "No, no, I want to call you. Every time I call the office, she sends someone else."

"Yeah, I understand that. Okay, here's my number," I replied, not caring if he ever called me again.

I lied to him about my age. I told him I was twenty-five, but I was twenty-eight. Plus, I didn't tell him I was a mother, because it was none of his business. However, when he walked me to my car, which had a car seat in the back, he didn't ask or say anything about it. That's on him if he didn't bring it up.

I was still working in Portland when he called a couple of weeks later, acting like he wanted to spend personal time with me. In my mind, work comes first.

I said, "Well, I have to work. I'm still working. I got a show to do."

"I want to see you," he replied. "I have time."

I said, "Well, that is not going to work."

"I'll pay you," he replied.

"You wanna pay me to hang out with me and take me to lunch? Like work?" I asked.

"Yeah," he replied.

"Oh, okay," I said. "I can do that."

So, he was paying me to go out to lunch and whatnot. Then, he would call me to talk to me about his wife's drama. I've never been married, but he was willing to listen to the advice I was giving him, putting in that extra thought, time, and details surrounding the circumstances.

For example, he would tell me how she kept spending his money all the time, so I said, "Geez, she sounds like a fucking handful. If she continues to spend your money, cut her credit cards in half. "

So, he did. I was like, holy shit! He asked me for advice all the time, and it became more like we were talking, rather than hanging out, with a lot of phone conversations. I only saw him about once a month, but we spoke at least four or five times a day. When I saw him, he showered me with thousands of dollars' worth of gifts with designer labels, most of which I had never heard of, such as a Louis Vuitton purse. The second time I met him, he bought me a Rolex. Then he bought me a house. I have fifty-nine Louis Vuitton bags, nine high-end watches, and tons of other gifts. I would see him every Wednesday at 10, every other Saturday, and whenever his wife was on vacation with the kids.

One day, he called me and asked, "How are you doing?"

I started crying and said, "My car had just been repossessed."

"Well, why don't you just go buy another one?" he asked.

"I don't have money or credit to do that," I replied. Surprisingly, he called me later that day and told me to go pick up my yellow Volkswagen Beetle at the local dealership. He was always lavishing me with gifts. When I first met him, he bought me a Rolex, then a house. I have fifty-nine Louis Vuitton bags, nine high-end watches, including a couple of Rolexes, and tons of other gifts. I would see him every Wednesday at 10 and every other Saturday when his wife was on vacation with the kids.

One day, he got caught at my house, and she hired a private detective to follow him. That is how his wife found out about our relationship. Then she filed for divorce. Going through their divorce, I was pulled into it because it is illegal to have an affair in New Hampshire if you are married. She tried to put me in jail, but I was told never to say we had sex in New Hampshire, just in Maine. It was the largest profile case in the state of New Hampshire, and millions of dollars were spent during this divorce.

Once the divorce was finalized, he still wanted me in his life, but from there, there was a custody hearing, which involved his ex-wife trying to say that I was unfit to be around his kids. And also, unworthy to be around my own son.

Now, I had to prove to the state of New Hampshire that I was a wonderful mother and fit to be around children. Once, I worked as a nanny and knew how to entertain kids and be around them appropriately. During that custody hearing, I was watching his son and making him strawberry shortcake when I got a phone call out of the blue from his father.

He said, "You've got to leave the house immediately."

"What?" I asked in disbelief.

He said, "Drive to Tennessee, and stay there until I tell you it is safe to come back."

My sister lives in Tennessee, so without hesitation, I panicked, ran home to pack a bag, grabbed my son, jumped in my car, and left immediately. It wasn't until I was two states away that I questioned myself and realized what I was doing. Mentally, I had faded out again while I was driving.

By the time I arrived in Tennessee, I felt overwhelmed with stress, anxiety, sadness, and confusion about why I had to leave. I wasn't given any explanation for my sudden departure from him or his house. Since his son was only eight years old at the time, he told me to leave his son alone. That made it clear how urgent it was for me to leave immediately. I remember him telling me, "Leave him there. Just get out."

Later, I found out that the authorities were planning to subpoena me to testify against him in his custody hearing because I was at his house in New Hampshire. I had to stay at my sister's house for three months because I wasn't allowed to go back, not even to Maine, since I would have to drive through New Hampshire to get there. He had me convinced that the police would set up roadblocks along the way, and for some reason, I believed him. I trusted him because he was an intelligent man and someone with an educational background.

When I would call him crying and ask him when I could come home, I realized then that I was no longer the supportive girlfriend, but more of a liability and burden to him. He didn't want me in his life, even though he liked me and enjoyed hanging out with me. The only reason he kept me close was that he didn't want me to open my mouth. He didn't want someone to approach me and ask questions because, after hanging out with me for those four years, he knew my first instinct is to tell the truth. It isn't to lie. If I were to be questioned without him being present, he was afraid of what I would say.

For years, I was never, ever allowed to tell people who he was, what his name was, or what he did for a living. People thought I was making up my relationship with him because we kept it extremely private. It was just him and me. Mind you, I am not complaining; it was perfect for a while. But after the divorce and the custody hearing, it became the complete opposite and a nightmare for me. We wouldn't go out in public together in town. When he would take me on vacation, he would dress me in slutty outfits, something he was adamant about and expected.

Raising my son, I got used to dressing modestly, but now I was dating a man who didn't want me to look modest in any way. When the custody hearing was over, I returned home and discovered he got full custody of his kids. It turned out that his wife, the mother of his children, was molesting his children. He knew it and allowed it never saying anything until it was used against her in the court of law. He admitted in court that he watched his wife masturbate his daughter when she was 4 years old. Both he and the nanny watched, but neither one called the authorities. He also started sleeping with his daughter in that bed, watching porn, while his daughter would lie on top of him, or he would lie on his daughter. To this day, his daughter has tried to have sex with him twice as a teenager.

Definitely confused, she asked, "Daddy. Why won't you let me lie on you now? Why won't you lie on me? I want to have sex with you, I have needs, is it because I got fat?"

He didn't care that she had gained weight as a teenager, but he said, "No, no. You're my daughter."

"Well, it didn't matter when I was a kid," she replied. "And I'm still your daughter."

He said, "No."

To this day, she hates me because I'm skinny, and she's heavy, and her father wouldn't sleep with her, but he was sleeping with me. She would bang on the bedroom door while we were being intimate.

"Hurry up and fuck her, Dad! Hurry up and get off! Hurry up! You don't need to be fucking her this long," she yelled through the door.

Through all that, I still had to perform. I wasn't allowed to get up off him to go tell her to move from the door to leave, or I would get in trouble. I would be the problem. So, I let this out-of-control teenager scream at the door, but he would still be fucking me! It wouldn't faze him at all! Then I would have to leave that room, acting as if that's normal, but nothing about that household was normal.

While we were dating, I discovered that his daughter gave her brother two blowjobs. She told her father and me about it. She said that she was horny and needed to practice, so she blew her brother. Nothing was done about. He didn't check on his son, nor did he tell his daughter that it was wrong. He was oblivious to the whole situation. When she told me,

I dropped what I had in my hand.

My first reaction was," Oh my God. I am shocked. What do we do? Should we go check on him? He's only six. You know, what do we do?"

She was only twelve and four years older than her brother, so his first blowjob from his sister was when he was six, and the second one happened when he was thirteen. His mother gave him a hand job at his second birthday party in front of everyone, calling it a little pickle, and he got an erection because she kept playing with it. When I read all the court documents from his computer after their divorce that he showed me, it was disgusting. Their parents sexually molested them, but it was treated as if it were normal.

Immediately, I was curious to know if either one of the parents had been molested as a child themselves. His wife is from the Pakistani culture, and it was common for her male relatives, uncles, her brother, and her dad to have sex with her. When she was married to her husband, she showered with her father, and he would catch her in the shower with her father. One day, her father got in the shower with him and demanded to see his penis erect because he wanted to see what his daughter was enjoying in sexual pleasure. Amazingly, he went along with it.

When he told me about it, I said, "I'm not that type of person. That's wrong and disgusting. That's inappropriate. You can't do that."

While dating him, his daughter would sit on his lap as a teenager, watching sexually driven movies together, while I would sit beside him. She would start by sitting on the other side of him, but eventually make her way onto his lap, hugging and holding him.

Again, I told him what I thought and said, "That's inappropriate. That's okay when she's 4 or 5, but not when she's 17, 18, or 19. This is weird." But whenever I would speak my mind, I would get in trouble.

He would say something like, "Oh, you're just jealous. You're just jealous, Deanna.

"No, I'm not jealous at all. I don't get jealous of children," I replied. "I don't get jealous of anyone."

But they were inappropriate all the time. The movies that they watched together were very sexual, so my son and I would have to leave the living room because it was inappropriate for what they were watching. I don't watch movies with my son that show women with their boobies out. He is my son, but that wasn't uncommon in that house. While I was dating him, I disagreed with what was going on. The only way I could handle the situation was to separate it from my daily activities, because he was giving me a weekly allowance and had to be at his beck and call. I had to take his calls and go to his house when he wanted. I was at his home at 7:30 in the morning and would stay there until 5 pm, Monday through Friday, to take care of his kids. But I was still his girlfriend, and I was getting paid.

On the weekends, I wasn't allowed at his house at all, because that's when he had special time with his kids. Besides, I didn't want to be there anyway after spending a whole week with them. I needed a break. It was a job to me. I was the nanny who had to serve the father and the kids. Meanwhile, I was getting paid $3,000 or $4,000 a week, which allowed me to pay my bills, and my son was doing okay.

When Friday night rolled around, I would ask him for more money, which was something he didn't give me a hard time about. But if I told him that he hurt my feelings because of what he said, I would get in trouble. If I needed $10,000, he would give it to me without needing an explanation for why I needed the money. Early in our relationship, I learned that it was easy for him to shut people up by paying them. Since he spent money entertaining his kids on the weekend, I thought to myself, "Why don't I do the same?" So now, I was receiving eight to ten grand a week.

However, I had no idea that what was happening would affect my son and me in the long run. I had no idea that my son was witnessing me having a relationship that was so toxic and unhealthy that he would never want one of his own. I continued doing what I thought I was doing well by him, by bringing home money and being happy when I was around him.

That said, I would cry a lot in my car because of the things that my boyfriend and his children would say to me, like, "Oh, she's just a whore," or "She's white trash. "Why are you fucking her dad? Is it because she's skinny? She's not even nice. She's not even pretty? You can get someone prettier. She's anorexic, obviously, she's not healthy. She's not happy. If she were happy, she'd eat." They would insinuate all kinds of horrible things about me and say it openly, and I wasn't to react or respond to anything. I was told to stand over in the corner, and they would let me know when they needed me. Without realizing this absurd behavior, I went and stood in the fucking corner!

When my boyfriend came out of the master bedroom an hour or two later, he asked me, "What are you doing?"

"I'm just standing here," I said. "I'm just standing here waiting to be needed until 5 o'clock, till I can leave. I don't want to get yelled at anymore."

While I was watching his kids, they ate a lot. My son and I don't indulge. I would have to go to restaurants and get them takeout food, because they got what they wanted every day. And these were high-end, full-course meals from high-end restaurants. When their father got home, they would tell their father that they were hungry, that they hadn't eaten all day. They would say things like, "Deanna doesn't eat and doesn't feed us. She won't feed us dad because she doesn't eat either."

Again, I got in trouble because he would call me and say, "Why don't you feed my fucking kids? Don't I give you enough fucking money? What the fuck are you even here for?"

"Wait, what? What are you talking about? Of course, I feed them. I go to the Texas Roadhouse and Applebee's all the time for you. I go to the wharf downtown, and they get steaks and salads," I said.

"Well, Destin said, "I'm always hungry, Daddy." When are you coming home? Because she won't feed me. She won't feed us at all."

That's when I started taking photos on my phone of every meal I served them, so when their father called to say I wasn't feeding them anymore, I sent him the pictures of all the meals I had fed them that week. Well, guess what? That backfired on me, because now they were saying to him, "Is she taking pictures of all the food she's feeding us because she's skinny and she thinks we're fat? Is she trying to body shame us, Dad?

When I heard this, I said, "No! Did you let them know it's because they constantly lie?" I had to defend myself all the time and show proof.

He said, "No, why would I do that?"

I said, "You don't want to shame them. You won't shame your children."

He never tells them no. His daughter switched schools three times because she was extremely sexually active, performing oral acts of pleasure at school and getting caught. Then she would get embarrassed, and Daddy would have to fix it, and move her to another school. After moving to three different high schools, she ended up having to go into a mental hospital after being diagnosed as a nymphomaniac. Unfortunately, she sexually assaulted five patients at that mental hospital, forcing them to move her to another state. If she were a man, she would have been arrested, but she was considered a predator.

I have four nephews and on occasion, they would come to visit us at different times. His daughter would stand naked in her bedroom door, hoping that they would walk by and see her naked. And then she would act all innocent and say something like, "Oh, you just saw my boobies. You weren't supposed to see my boobies and then ask them, "What did you think about my boobies? Are they cute?" She was playing victim but wanted their reaction. After that incident, I never brought my nephews back for a visit.

I told my son every time we went to his house, "You are not allowed in a room alone with her. If she asks you any questions about her body, you say you don't know. Don't answer yes or no. It's a setup." Her brother couldn't have friends over because they would wake up, and she would be giving them a blowjob. I walked in on them at 4 o'clock in the morning. She was in bed with her brother, giving a blow job to his friend. They were in 8th grade, and she was in high school.

Immediately, I went downstairs to tell her father what I had just seen, and now I was considered the troublemaker. That is why my son is not allowed near his daughter at all. She taught my son the word vagina after purposely telling her not to teach my son any words, because her mouth is vulgar. It's worse than any child speaking like that, but the words that were coming out of her mouth were clitoris, vagina, penetration, come, and orgasm. These are words that she was saying to my son while he was in elementary and middle school, and she was in high school.

"I don't teach him those words," I said to her.

Well, he knows vagina," she replied.

I said, "Who taught him that?"

She was insinuating that I had taught him that. She didn't know what kind of mother I was, but I wasn't anything like her mother. I never taught my son that word. I never once said that word around my son, let alone say it out loud. She is a monster.

6

A PUZZLE - WHY I STAYED

I'll admit the money wowed me. I had never seen that much money before in my life, and to come in so easily, all I had to do was ask. I have seen people work from 3 AM until 10 PM and not make anything close to the amount of money I have seen in an hour.

Knowing that I had to deal with this as a bad job, I literally told him one day, "I just look at this as work."

"You do?" he replied.

"Yeah, doesn't everybody hate their job?

"No. You hate coming here?" he asked, looking surprised.

"Well, why would I enjoy it?" I asked. "It's terrible. Your children are mean to me."

"Well, that's not good," he replied, not sure how to answer me.

I then realized that he didn't want to hear how it made me feel. That's why I would get in the car and cry every day when I left the house! I couldn't tell him what they were saying to me on a daily basis. He would blatantly tell me, "I don't want to fucking hear it. Learn to choose your battles with the kids." It was awful hearing the derogatory words coming out of their mouths. Even though I hated the job, I was getting paid good money for being there.

When it was just him and me, it was so different. He always treated and acted towards me as someone special. For example, he would say nice things to me like, "You know I love you," or "You're great." He would always refer to me as his 'little love, his soulmate.' That warmed my heart hearing those words.

One day, I asked him, "Why do you like me?"

It was then that he told me that I was a complicated burden and the whore who never left him during his divorce. In other words, he didn't know how to get rid of me, because I didn't leave him. He thought I would be scared off by the divorce, but he needed me—or so I thought. He just wanted to keep me close so that I would keep his secrets.

I thought he wanted me near him and his kids because he knew how great a nanny I was, how good a mother I was, how well I could teach his kids. I could say no to them. I could help them be a better person, like my son, but that's not what they wanted. They wanted to be entertained and served. I realized that's all I had to do: keep them entertained and serve them, not show any emotion, and leave. Get my money and go. Then, after crying my eyes out on my way home, I could enjoy the rest of my day with my son. I would put the money in the bank and pay my bills. Our lives were private, and my boyfriend was not part of my private life. I literally kept my personal life separate from him.

He had become a mean boss, and he cheated on me several times while we were dating. But because of how I met him, in my mind, I thought, well, I met him when he was married. Obviously, he said he wasn't intimate with his wife, but they all lie, of course, he was. It didn't bother me then that he was intimate with his wife, and I was just a whore. Well, now that I'm the girlfriend, am I still the whore? Can he still cheat on me? Can he still be with other women? Those are the questions I would ask myself.

Maybe it is okay. Perhaps I'm overreacting or putting too much thought into him sleeping with other women. It didn't bother me because I didn't like him. The entire time I was helping him raise his kids, I started to dislike him anyway: I just liked his money. He was attractive, the money was good, he was still giving me gifts, and he was financially providing for me.

One day, I said to him, "All you do for me is financially support me. You don't talk to me about my problems. We can't chit-chat about your daily goings on. We can't talk about anything."

"Well, what's that? Why would we have to?" he asked.

I said, "Because that's what people do. It's called conversation. Communication."

At that moment, I was shocked because, for the first time, I felt more intelligent than him as I explained something that seemed like common sense, but he was acting like it was a foreign concept. Sure. I stayed with him because, in the long run, if he weren't my boyfriend, he would be a good man. He does not know how to treat women, however. I actually felt sad for him because of how his children disrespected, talked to, and treated him. They are mean. They didn't just speak to me poorly; they also spoke poorly to their parents, and they took it. I didn't want to take it either, but I had to be there.

I also saw them calling him a drunk or saying things to him like, "You're going to hell," and "You're dating a whore. God doesn't love you, and you made our childhoods horrible. You never give me anything I need."

What his children said to him was horrible, which made me feel bad for him. I knew his children would run over him more if I weren't there. I felt like I was protecting him a little bit by staying there, not realizing that I was fucking up my own self in the long run. That is why I stayed out of compassion, money, and pity.

Dating him was like a nightmare of a puzzle, sprinkled with sugar, here and there, just keeping me interested enough to keep putting the puzzle together. However, I was never good at puzzles or word problems. When he would talk to me, it was like I had to solve a word problem because his actions never matched his words. I was always on guard, trying to figure out what he meant, what he would ask me, or trying to figure out what he just said. It confused me because he was an educated man, and I wasn't.

He would ask me simple questions about whether I was hungry, but I was never hungry because I knew I couldn't be. He didn't like it if I gained weight or ate in front of him, as he was always worried about my figure. When he asked me about it, I knew he was hungry. He was pretending, as if I needed him to figure out how to feed me. I would suggest places to eat, like Chick-fil-A or Smitty's, but he would look at me with disgust. We would always end up eating at the restaurant he chose. I was okay with that.

However, I always felt awkward entering a restaurant that I wasn't familiar with or that he suggested because the waitress would always give me the strangest look. At the time, I didn't realize that he was taking me to restaurants he went to alone, where he would flirt with the waitresses and act single. I felt uncomfortable without him realizing that he had just brought me to the place where he would be the bachelor. I felt like I had to compete with the wait staff for my position with him. When I felt confident with my appearance and myself, he would immediately notice and make me feel like shit. He would crack jokes with the wait staff, while I sat there feeling sad and not saying a word.

At that moment, I realized I needed to separate the social from the working part of our relationship, as I wasn't allowed to talk about him to anyone. I knew my neighbors thought I was imagining or making up our relationship. Some would tease me, questioning if I was lying about my exciting social life. After his divorce, he wanted me to stay around and said to me, "I will take you out in public, as long as you look cute and thin." I continued to work for him under his command, not as his girlfriend, but as his nanny and his whore.

At the beginning of what I thought was dating him, I took a trip with my son out of state. Driving back home, I had to pee so bad, and knowing my own health, I knew I would pass out if I held my urine any longer, so I stopped at his house to use the bathroom. When I arrived, I entered the private gate and was surprised to see that he was having a party. Immediately, I thought, 'What is happening here? Why wasn't I invited? Who are all these people?' I saw his brother, his wife, their child, and his children. People from his work were there, and other people I didn't know. He immediately ran over to me when he saw me, noticing my sad face and confusion.

When he made me feel this way, it was hard for me not to show my emotions on my face.

I asked him, "What are you doing?"

He said with a big smile on his face, "I'm having a party, Angel!"

I couldn't believe what was happening and felt my body become empty.

"Why wasn't I invited?" I asked. "Why weren't my son and I invited?" not allowing him to answer the first question.

He looked at me with dark eyes and said, "Because it's only for friends and family."

I started to cry. By this time, some of his guests began coming up to him while he was talking to me. When he saw them approaching us, he kissed me and said, "Excuse me. Angel, give me a kiss now."

I said "No."

Then he got mad at me because I didn't show him affection in front of his friends. I didn't allow him to think that everything was perfect at that moment, so I left. Later that night, he called me and asked, "Why are you so upset about the party? I'm allowed to throw parties and have friends over."

"I'm your girlfriend," I said. "Why wasn't I invited?"

No matter what I said, he still didn't see my point. It was becoming increasingly difficult for me to express my feelings.

He finally ended our conversation, and I said, "I need to take some time off."

"Why? Are you having your period?" he asked. "Why don't you go home for a few days until it's over and come back until you know how to talk to me?" and hung up the phone.

I needed to think about what I was going to tell him the next time I saw him. He would always say that to me if I shared my opinion or feelings. I started lying to him when I had something to say. I would tell him I was on my period, so at least I could express myself. I would make up an excuse for the opinion, knowing I'd get punished for it. I went home, took a few days off, and looked at it as if it were a vacation from not having to be around him or his kids.

I spent Valentine's Day with him and his daughter, because his daughter insisted that Valentine's Day was a daddy-daughter holiday. When I spoke up and said it wasn't, it was for people who date or are in a couple. She said I was wrong. I told her it was for people who were intimate with each other. She was sixteen, so I thought it was appropriate to explain it to her.

She said, "How dare you talk to me about being intimate with my father?"

She kept saying that it was inappropriate for me to compare my dating her dad with her relationship and love that she wanted and desired from her father. I didn't realize until later that his daughter actually had a sexual agenda with her father. She attempted to have sex with him twice in the middle of the night, asking him to penetrate her because she had needs that her father could fulfill for her.

He immediately threw his daughter off him, yelling, "What are you doing? What are you trying to do?"

She said, "Why won't you make love to me? Why?" Confused, she asked him, "Is it because I'm not thin like your girlfriend?"

He replied, "No, it's because you're my fucking daughter."

When she was little, her father would lie on her entire body, comforting her. She enjoyed feeling his body from head to toe on top of hers. She didn't know as a child that while this was happening, it was inappropriate. Now, as a teen, she required the same satisfaction of feeling that pleasure.

"You fucked De-De, she's skinny. Is it because she's skinny? You won't fuck me because I'm not skinny? I have needs, too, Dad," she insisted.

He replied again, "No, it's because you're my fucking daughter."

It happened only twice, twice too many, which was enough. Once on vacation in Miami and another time at his home. All I could do was take his word for it, because he texted me each time it occurred. I could only suggest things to say to her, knowing he would never discipline her or explain it to her in depth, that it was inappropriate and wrong. I told him all he could do was to lock all the doors to the entrance to his bedroom, which had three doors. On family vacations, she was old enough now to stay in her own room and had her own key. So that's what he did.

We knew that she had become extremely sexual as she got older. She performed oral sex on her brother, once when he was a young boy, under the age of eight, and then another time when he was thirteen. She told her father and me each time she had put her brother's penis in her mouth and pleasured him, saying it was fun as she told us the story about what she had done. Her father looked shocked but didn't say anything. I was stunned, too. However, nothing was ever done about that situation at home, because he didn't want to shame her. It was a big deal to him and his kids never to be shamed or held accountable for their actions, no matter how distraught and devilish they were. Finally, I convinced him that what she was doing was wrong.

I said to him, "If a man were doing what she was doing, he would be charged with gross sexual assault."

Eventually, he got her professional help, putting her in a hospital that helps nymphomaniacs. However, while she was there, she climbed on three male patients while they were sleeping, trying to get them to penetrate her. All that happened within the first week. Her dad was devastated and humiliated by this situation with his daughter and how she was behaving in public.

He moved her to another hospital/school where she could be treated for her illness and also get an education. She ended up assaulting one young lady in that school, but the school handled it differently, explaining to her that what she did was wrong, and no matter her feelings, she had to understand that the other person didn't enjoy her touching her. Still confused, she demanded that she had feelings and needs, and they were to be fulfilled.

Despite my efforts to try to help, I had to choose my battles. Every day was a battle. Every hour was a nightmare or a new lie that I had to defend myself against. It was extremely exhausting. However, he would somehow reassure me that he loved me, that I was his true love, and that he always wanted me to be there. I learned to hold on to those little moments.

Although they became fewer and fewer, the years had passed without my realizing that it had become a decade.

One day, I called my sister and said, "I hate him. I fucking hate him. I can't take it anymore. I want out. It's not fun anymore."

"Fake it until you make it," she replied.

"I never heard that before," I said to her, confused. "What are you talking about?"

She said, "I fake it until I make it," and reassured me that I could do the same. She also reminded me that she still needed me for the money I got from him because she was financially struggling, and I always helped her by providing for her kids through my allowance from him.

Since I didn't want to disappoint her or her two sons, I kept doing what I needed to do. I became mentally strong enough to take his bullshit along with his insults and continued acting like I was happy with my situation. I would put on my big girl panties, preparing myself for another day of dating him, and taking care of his children, always looking for the bigger prize, the money. The money was always there, the one consistent thing that I could count on and grew to rely on.

That said, it was so frustrating dealing with his daughter, who would consistently lie about me. She knew how to take and flip my comments and was extremely smart. For example, when I had to take my nephews to get their wisdom teeth taken out, I took a picture of them because their cheeks were chubby like a chipmunk's.

When she had her wisdom teeth removed, I put her to bed in her room upstairs and took a picture of her. I thought, "Wow, look how cute! They look like chipmouths!" While she was lying there, looking like a chubby little chipmunk with her face swollen, I went and got her brother and showed him his sister.

"Is she alright?" he asked.

"Yes, she's fine, she's just sleeping," I replied.

"Her face is chubby. It's swollen," he noticed.

"Yes, it's because her wisdom teeth were pulled. The swelling will go down eventually. Doesn't she look like a chubby little chipmunk?" I asked.

The next day, I showed her the picture I had taken of her cute face; it was all swollen and looked like a chipmunk. Well, that got thrown in my face because I was accused of calling her fat and being a creep by taking pictures of a child who was asleep in her bed. Realizing what I had been charged with, I tried to explain my actions to no avail. It was too much for me to deal with. I was finally done. I told her father I no longer want to be around his kids, that they were entitled, disrespectful, lying, soulless monsters.

He agreed and yelled, "Oh, honey, I can't take them either. They're so horrible. What the fuck are we supposed to do?"

"I don't know," I replied.

"I can't believe their behavior. I don't understand why my children act this way. I never wanted fucking kids. They get this from their fucking mother," he screamed. "I should've never knocked her up."

I tried to reassure him that if we both started disciplining them now and showing them structure, they could become good adults. That wasn't what he wanted to hear. He knew it was a lot easier just to let them have their way and say yes to their demands without putting any limits on them.

His daughter asked the babysitter to buy her a dildo, and when the babysitter told her she couldn't, she had the babysitter fired. The second babysitter did buy her the dildo and told us all about it, but that babysitter didn't get fired. This was something that was supposed to be normal.

He said to me, "I told the babysitter not to buy her sex toys anymore."

When she demanded that she buy her a sex toy, or she would get her fired, too, the babysitter felt threatened. Every day, there was something I could have pointed out to him that was inappropriate.

On another occasion, I caught his children kissing with open mouths in the pool using tongue.

I called my sister and asked her, "What do I do? He won't believe me if I tell him?"

Then I thought about recording them to show him, but then I would be accused of being a sexual predator, and I didn't want my son near this either, so I told my son to get out of the pool. I allowed his children to continue doing what they were doing, knowing that it was disgusting, but I didn't want to get in trouble later either.

Later that night, when their father got home, I told him what I saw, and of course, he got mad at me and said I was a troublemaker. He asked me to take my son and go home, which I did. Later that weekend, he called me to apologize because he was witnessing the same thing I had seen a few days earlier. His children were making out in the pool. He didn't know what to do.

I told him, "As their father, you need to tell them right now that it's wrong and it's inappropriate, and they are never to do that again."

He said he would talk to them about their behavior, but it was turned back on me for bringing it up the first time. Another mindfuck that I could never win.

7

MENTAL HOSPITAL 2008

In 2008, at his son's birthday, my boyfriend had no idea the mental and emotional abuse that I was dealing with. I honestly had no idea myself. I had heard of sexual and physical abuse, and I had been abandoned, but I'd never heard of mental and emotional abuse. I had no idea that those existed. I had no idea that dating him would cause me to end up admitting myself into a mental hospital on his son's birthday.

I woke up that morning, walked to an office building in my town, and crawled underneath a woman's desk. While I was under her desk, I asked her to get me a blanket and a pillow so I could rest. She did as I asked. Meanwhile, she took the time to search for who I was to see if I had a mental illness, and finally found my doctor, who was in a building next door.

The kind woman walked me over to my doctor, and that's when my doctor told me that I had fallen off the edge that day, and I needed to be admitted to a mental hospital so that she could help me. I agreed but said I had to call my boyfriend and tell him that I wasn't going to be at his house that night for his son's birthday and that I was being admitted into a mental hospital.

I never told my boyfriend anything about me or my personal life; frankly, he didn't want to know anyway, and I knew this, so I kept all my traumas to myself that I was dealing with. My doctor was confused when speaking to him because the only thing he asked was, "Did she pick up his cake? Did she pick up my son's birthday cake? Or do I have to pick it up myself?"

"I couldn't do it," I said, jumping into the conversation. I heard the disappointment in his voice.

"Fine. I'll pick up the cake myself," he said, rather annoyed.

I tried to explain to him that I had a nervous breakdown, but he didn't want to hear it. It was at that moment that I realized that I was putting myself through hell, dating him, and helping him raise his children. It made my situation worse. He just wanted me for sex and didn't care about me personally. I knew I had to get to the hospital right away. I didn't speak to him for a few days, but that was okay for me. Since I knew his passcode on his answering machine, I would dial it to see if anyone was calling him outside of our relationship.

He got a call from a young girl saying, "Honey, I can't meet you at 10 today. I'll have to meet you at 10:15. My roommate is borrowing my car."

I was sad after listening to that message, and that's when I started putting the tracker on his vehicle once I got out of the mental hospital. Knowing that I was admitted there because of all the bullshit that I endured in this relationship, I was devastated, but I didn't tell him what I knew and just went about my day, hoping I would get better. He came to visit me once, bringing sneakers and some chips, making me feel like he was my boyfriend, and reassuring me that I would get better and that he loved me.

He wouldn't come and get me when I was checked out 10 days later. He had my niece drive 2 hours out of her way to pick me up and drop me off at his house. When I arrived, he was on the phone with a girl with whom he spoke for 45 minutes before he would even hug me or acknowledge that I was home from the mental hospital.

When he got off the phone, I went to embrace him, and he stepped back and said, "Ugh. You need to take a shower. You smell like that place."

He should talk. At the end of his relationship with his 20-year-old girlfriend, he contracted a sexually transmitted disease (STD), specifically herpes, something he could also get in his line of work. If you have such a disease, you have to tell your patients and your staff so you and they can make the surroundings more comfortable and sterile. For example, if a person has AIDS, they are required to tell the patient, "I have AIDS, and if you don't want me to work on you, it's up to you." The same applies to herpes because it is a contagious disease.

For the safety and the well-being of others, my boyfriend asked me if he could prescribe the medication in my name, not his. He had the means to write prescriptions, so he wrote his prescription for his herpes in my name, so no one would know he had it. It didn't matter to him that when I went to the pharmacy to pick up the prescription, it was embarrassing for me. I thought, well, he was the one in the medical field, and I was just the poor whore, so why not help him out?

When he explained to me how he got the STD, it was from his previous girlfriend, but he still wanted to have sex with me. I was scared knowing a little bit about herpes, because my sister had contracted the same STD from her first fiancé. I knew that it was painful and extremely itchy, and that the vagina would swell up. I didn't want that for me. He assured me that if I had sex with him three days after the outbreak, I would not contract the disease. I still questioned his explanation for me not to get the disease because he then explained to me that his brother also had herpes and that he had never given it to his former wife while being sexually active for seventeen years. That gave me validation to believe him.

When I think about my earlier life, it was so sad, and I never had a support system. I started going to therapy after being discharged from the mental hospital in 2008, and the therapist asked me about my support group.

I looked at her and asked, "What support group?" I didn't know what it meant, and I am not afraid to ask because I need to know. "I don't know what that means," I said to her. I thought she was asking if I went to group classes.

She said, "Do you have people in your family or in your life that you can talk to, and that you can go to?

I said, "Yes," mainly because I was too embarrassed to say no, but the truth was, I didn't have anyone. I never had a support team. After that session, I got in my car and just cried my eyes out. I never had anyone say to me, "You want someone to talk to? Call me." I tell people all the time, I might not be able to help you, but you know what? I can make you laugh

8

LEAN AND THIN

My boyfriend liked me lean and thin, something he constantly expressed in our relationship. After a few years of dating him, I felt comfortable and confident in myself, and thought I would put on 3 to 5 pounds to get some curvy hips and a little butt, but he didn't like that I put on the weight. He sent me home and told me to take the time I needed to take the weight off, and that he would buy me an elliptical to help me get back into shape. Sure enough, the elliptical arrived, and it took me two weeks to tone up and get back to my perfect little frame.

I never wanted to be a bad girl or annoy him in any way, but sometimes it didn't matter to me. I was going to say what was on my mind either way. So this particular time, I said what I had to say and pissed him off. Like so many times before, he told me, "Leave now and don't come back until you know how to speak to me correctly."

I said, "All I'm doing is talking to you like your kids talk to you. What's the difference?"

He told me, "Get out."

I told him to fuck off. When I left, his son called me and said, "Don't leave when Dad tells you to leave. He's just starting a fight with you over nothing so that another girl can come over."

I asked him, "What are you talking about?"

"Every time you leave, after you and Dad fight, another girl comes over," he said again.

That devastated me to hear those words, and I knew his son wasn't lying, because he didn't want me there anyway. He was hoping that I would take that information to heart and leave his father. I would have the arsenal to throw back in his father's face, which would destroy our relationship, finally. But that's not what I did. I put a tracker on his vehicle, and in a few weeks, it picked up where he was going. What his son told me was true. It was right in my face. He had met a 23-year-old stripper in another club in Massachusetts. He was in his mid-60s, and his girlfriend was twenty-four, a year younger than his own daughter.

I actually followed him from July to January of 2017, and on New Year's Eve Day, the first day of 2018, I told him, "Hey, I want to show you something. I can't go on this way anymore."

"What are you talking about?" he asked.

"I know you're cheating on me," I said.

"No, I'm not," he insisted.

"I know you have a girlfriend. I have proof," I said emphatically.

"No, you don't," he replied.

"Yes, I do. I'll show you," I said. I took out my phone and showed him the photos I had of him at restaurants, T-Mobile, and the mall, where he was buying her furniture for her new apartment. He grabbed my phone out of my hand, deleted the photos, and said, "I see nothing, I don't know what you're talking about."

I couldn't believe it. I looked at him with so much confidence and said, "Hey, I'm lucky that I at least emailed those photos to myself," and showed him the photos a second time. That's when it hit him like a target, but I wasn't allowed the prize. He kept looking at me, confused, wondering how I could be so clever and smart enough to figure out what he had been up to on my own, being so uneducated and poor.

After that conversation, I left and went to a football game with two of my friends in Gillette Stadium. Later that night, I got a call from him accusing my dog of biting his friend. I got extremely worried because he is the type who would have a dog put down without any questions, whereas I'm the type of person who will go to jail for my pets. There's no doubt that he knew that by accusing my dog of biting, it would stress me out, but I was scared he was going to kill him. The ride home from the game was intense, and my friends tried calming me down, but it didn't help.

When I got to the house, I said, "Where's your friend? Where is he? Where's my dog? Where did he bite him? Let me see. He didn't bite him at all." The questions just kept flowing out of me, and I wanted answers. I wanted them immediately.

When I saw his friend, I said, "I was told my dog bit you. My dog weighs 140 pounds. If he bit you, you would have broken skin." He showed me his sweater. There was nothing wrong. My dog didn't bite him. He didn't do anything. It was a lie.

I asked his friend, "Were you scared of my dog?"

He said, "No."

I said, "So this was all bullshit. It was a lie. My dog didn't even get near you, did he?"

My boyfriend just wanted to ruin my day and make sure I didn't have fun with my friends. I was so angry when I realized what was going on. I grabbed his friend, and I scared the shit out of him. I yelled, "Are you fucking scared of me? You should be, asshole. You lied about my dog." My dog and my friends just stood there, thinking, "Wow," and feeling embarrassed, yet again.

I was still helping my boyfriend raise his two children while he was married before his divorce, and though he had four nannies help raise his children, now, it was my responsibility to be the nanny and the whore. My boyfriend didn't really want any part in raising his children. He always said, "I didn't want kids. She did," meaning their mother. She wanted to have the children so she could get child support if he ever left her. They always fought over the money she spent, and she would spend a lot. Her father had convinced her to get herself knocked up to keep that money coming in.

When we discussed not wanting his kids, I would gently tell him, "You got them now. I know plenty of people who aren't financially stable and didn't plan on being parents, but they stepped up, and you could be a good parent, too. And I am one of them."

My son has a form of autism, and he would always ask me, "How come others can do something and I can't? Why do you tell them yes and me no?"

I would always tell him, "Honey, it's because mommy told you no for your own good. I'd have to tell the other two "Yes," no matter what, whether it's good for them or not.

He said, "But they're doing bad things, and you're saying yes to them.

"I know, I've been asked by their father just to allow them to do whatever they want, and that he didn't even want to hear about it," I replied.

It would always fall on my lap, but I reassured my son that I was raising him for society and for the future. People would like him as an adult, welcome him into their home, and speak well of him once he leaves. My boyfriend's kids weren't going to be liked. They weren't going to be allowed in people's homes because they were bad news.

My son looked up to me and trusted my advice. All my decisions were in his best interest, so he never gave me a problem. When I had to tell him no a few times, even when he wanted to hear yes, his feelings were hurt, but he learned to understand that it was called discipline.

"It's good for you," I said.

There was never a second thought about disappointing my child. My boyfriend and I had planned a trip to New York for the three children, his two and my one. We were all going to try to do a family trip, at least that's what they called it. I never wanted to be part of their family because it was weird. However, I still wanted my son to experience the FAO Schwarz toy store in New York and the big M&M building we discussed for our trip. He was just as excited as my boyfriend's son (they are two weeks apart in age) to see the attractions and experience New York.

We spent the night at their house and planned on leaving early in the morning. After we had all packed up and were ready to go, the limo pulled up out front, and we started gathering our luggage to head out. Before opening the front door, my boyfriend stopped, turned, and looked at me, and announced in front of his children, "Oh, I'm sorry, you and your son can't come."

"What?" I asked in shock. "Why not? What's going on?" I was stunned and thought I had misheard what he had just said.

"Well, my daughter and I have decided that it's just going to be a family trip, and you aren't family, so you have to stay here," he said with a straight face.

At that horrible moment, I had to tell my son that he wasn't going to New York, and that he couldn't see the M&M Building or the famous toy store. It was put on my shoulders to disappoint my son while his children ran the show. They went on their trip, and while they were there, he called me several times, telling me how miserable it was, how it would have been much easier if I had gone with them to help him with his children.

Knowing how bad his children were, I still tried to explain that he told me we couldn't go. That is his way of manipulating me. After all, it wasn't my idea to stay home and disappoint my son. He then suggested that I accompany him and his children on vacations in the future but keep my son at home with a babysitter. I told him no. Despite how he treated me, I always felt bad when I wanted to break up with him. I didn't want to leave him alone with his kids, knowing that his daughter was actually harassing him.

Plus, his son was destroying his house by overflowing toilets with gallons of water, causing horrendous damage. Both children were dreadful. His son flooded the toilets every time he took a poo by using an entire roll of tissue that would be stuffed in the toilet, and then he let it run. Eventually, all the toilets overflowed, and he never shut the water off in the back. He would walk away, ruining twelve toilets throughout the house in the process.

Both children were beyond disrespectful towards both their parents. They would be rude and use foul language in restaurants while addressing other adults. I would constantly have to tell people that I'm not their mother, I'm just the nanny. They were spoiled rotten, and he would give them whatever they wanted, when they wanted. If they became unhappy with what they received, they would blame their parents for not giving in to their demands and for not being better parents at making better decisions for them. It was another mindfuck. I stopped taking it personally what his children did to me because I could see how they treated their own parents.

For example, they would call their mama drunk if she simply had a glass of wine during dinner. They would blame their dad for anything that didn't go well and say, "Well, Dad, you're a shitty dad for even letting us do it," or "You're a shitty dad for always giving in to us." It would always fall back on him, so I thought if I stuck around, it would help him be less stressed in his life. Honestly, the abuse from his children didn't matter to me. After being there for so long, I just got used to it. I hated seeing how they treated their father. To this day, it still bothers me.

I continued tracking him and discovered he wasn't going where he said he was going. Unfortunately, the day after Easter, he went and saw her, the other woman, and that night, I confronted him and said, "I know where you were today."

We had an argument about me following him, and that he felt that I was being sneaky and doing something unacceptable in our relationship, and that he couldn't trust me anymore, not to follow him. That's when he kicked me out. He no longer wanted me around. I was sad that I put all that time, effort, and emotion into helping him raise his kids and make his life what I thought was easier. Plus, I was financially being rewarded, but his cheating on me confused me a little bit because our sex life wasn't intimate; it was controlled.

We would have sex on Tuesday nights because he had Wednesdays off, and it would help him sleep in the next day. If, for some reason, we couldn't have sex on Tuesday night, I would have to be prepared to have sex on Wednesday morning. That meant a shower and a shave. I was always to be fully shaved if we were going to have sex.

He would ask me, "Did you shave today?"

My reply was always the same: "Yes, Daddy!"

Sex on the weekend depended on his mood if he was tired. I did try a couple of times to be intimate with him on our off days by wearing sexy, cute lingerie outside of the designated times. The first time was when the Red Sox baseball team was in the World Series. I wore socks, a baseball hat, and a tiny, revealing baseball jersey when he watched the game. When I came out into the living room, all happy and excited to show him what I had to offer him, he made me feel stupid.

"What are you wearing? What are you doing? You're making me feel uncomfortable in my own home," he exploded. "Go change. You know I'm not prepared or ready to have sex with you. Are you horny?"

"I just thought it would be fun if I looked cute for you during the game," I said.

"You're not," he said. "It's making me feel uncomfortable. You're making me feel pressured to have sex with you. I don't want to have sex with you."

"Okay," I replied. "No big deal." And off I went to change clothes.

The second time I wore lingerie, it was the night before we were flying home from a trip. I walked out of the bathroom wearing an outfit, and he burst out laughing.

"What are you wearing?" he asked.

"I'm a little stewardess. Aren't you interested at all?" I asked, making an effort to connect with him.

He told me, "Go and change."

I dressed up as a stewardess because he had told me how many times they turned him on as a younger man. Flying all over the country giving lectures, he often had one-night stands with stewardesses he met on the flights. Since it was his fantasy, I thought, why not give my boyfriend the fantasy he always wanted? Well, as it turned out, that wasn't what he wanted from me. He didn't want me to wear lingerie, and he made me feel unappreciated, unattractive, and unwanted.

Our sex life was never exciting. The first time he put his hands on my vagina, he looked at me, confused, and said, "You're wet."

I said, "Yeah, I'm supposed to be, right?" I was excited. Immediately, he went to the bathroom to wash his hands.

I thought to myself, "Oh my god, this is one of those guys who doesn't know that when a woman is turned on, her vagina gets moist." I never got moist again. And when I thought I was, I immediately would go into the bathroom and wipe it off until I was bone dry. He never put his hands on me during sex, but he would always put his left hand on my right hip. The first 10 years of having sex with him, I had to lie face down with a pillow under my stomach so that he could prop up my ass. When I found out he was cheating on me, I told him that I didn't care.

"You're probably fucking looking at her," I said to him, suddenly aggravated by the thought.

"What?" he asked, looking confused by my angry comment.

"Well, you're fucking her," I replied.

"What is that supposed to mean?" he asked, still befuddled.

So, I told him, "The first 10 years, you didn't even realize that you always fucked me face down. You wouldn't even look at me. So, I don't care who you're having sex with. I've been faking my orgasms for the last 10 years anyway."

"Well, I never complained about it," he replied.

I said, "Why would you? I gave you everything you wanted. I gave you everything." He just wanted to penetrate me, and I was embarrassed. I told him that he never gave me an orgasm, but when I said those words, I could see the light disappear in his face. After all, he thought of himself as the macho man and pleaser.

I continued having sex with him while he was with his new girlfriend. I don't know why, though he told me that he wanted to. I was still getting my allowance, so I looked at it as if I were working for him now. He honestly thought he was pleasuring me because he would make comments such as, "I made such great love to you today, honey, didn't I?"

And I would always say, "Yes, Daddy, you did, yes, you did," but I was faking it every time. He had no idea. He would call and have me come over after he hung up with her, but he complained to me about her several times because she was young, and she would overdose while using drugs like ecstasy and cocaine. Several times, she would overdose, and he would have to give her IVs instead of taking her to the hospital because of his occupation; he knew how to get the liquids and the needles for the IV. It would help her get through the overdosing or passing out and revive her. When he told me this, I was thinking, I'm underweight and tired, I want a bag of liquid.

"Why don't I get a bag of liquid?" I finally asked him.

"You don't use drugs or overdose," he replied.

"If I get sick with a cold or flu, could I please have a bag of fluids?" I asked with a smile.

He finally agreed and brought a bag of fluid to his house, where I would lie comfortably in a room he provided me. I kept thinking to myself, "Wow, here is another health benefit. This is his way of thanking me for staying with him. It wasn't money. But now I can be healthy." He was like my own private doctor.

Eventually, his relationship with his younger girlfriend didn't last long, just over a year. He finally left her in 2019 and continued to date me. At the same time, he was dating her and dating me, I realized that I was now the side chick. I went from whore to girlfriend to now side chick. It didn't matter as long as I was still getting my allowance and being financially supported.

When he left her in 2019, he admitted to me that she told him she was embarrassed to be seen with him since he was forty years older than her. She noticed people staring at them, but that was something one should never say to him. By this time, his kids were all grown up. He didn't have a girlfriend; it was just him and me, something I'd always worked to achieve. I finally accomplished it, something I set out to do years ago. I have a relationship with this handsome Italian man. Finally, dreams do come true.

One day, he surprised me with a trip to Chicago, one of my favorite cities. I love the hot dogs and how they put a pickle on them. They are delicious. While walking around downtown, I had a hot dog, and we ended up going to a jewelry store. It wasn't uncommon for us to pop into a jewelry store so he could look at the watches and other shiny, expensive things. But this time, it was different. He was asking me what I thought, what I liked.

While that may sound wonderful, it also triggered an unpleasant flashback from a time years ago, when we were dating and he asked me to bring a t-shirt on vacation that said, *"Girlfriend to Fiancé"* that I had found at Goodwill. We were on our way to Florida, and I brought the t-shirt to wear, and I was thinking, "Wow, friend to fiancé, this must mean I'm getting engaged." I'm going to be proposed to on our Florida trip this time, but that wasn't true.

While I was wearing the shirt, he said, "You look silly wearing that shirt."

"Silly? You're the one who told me to bring it," I replied.

"Yeah, I didn't expect you to wear it," he said with a scoff.

I was so embarrassed and said, "I'm wearing it because I thought you were going to propose to me."

"Propose to you? Why on earth would I do that?" he asked.

I was humiliated. I actually believed that he was going to marry me. Remembering… now, we were in Chicago, looking for diamonds, I really didn't hope anything would come out of it at all. I didn't want to ask any questions.

When he would ask me about a ring, I would say, "Yeah, I like that ring," or "Yeah, that is pretty." Just straightforward answers to his questions about the diamonds. There was one ring that really stood out to me: a gorgeous 5.3-carat diamond solitaire, but I still didn't think anything of it.

Unknowingly, while in Chicago, he purchased the ring that I picked out and surprised me with it in December of 2019. Wow. I was floored. I was the happiest girl in the world! Everything that he had done to me prior, everything that his kids had said to me, and did to me, was gone. It was immediately erased by this shiny diamond that I had in my hand. I felt like I had finally won the prize. However, what I received was not a prize at all.

9

NO PROPOSAL

There was no proposal. He never actually asked me to marry him. The ring had arrived at his office, and he came home with it, looking very excited about something. I had no idea what he was excited about.

He said, "I have something for you."

It could have been a new handbag or a new outfit. He loved buying me Louis Vuitton clothing, so it could have been anything. I wasn't expecting a diamond. We went upstairs into his bedroom, and he sat down on the edge of the bed and said, "Here, sit down, I want to show you something, I want to give you something."

In anticipation of what he had for me, I was very excited because I had never seen him so animated and enthusiastic. With a dry personality, he never showed excitement for much of anything.

A red box appeared, and he gently laid it in my hand. I unwrapped it, lifted the front end of the box, and there sat the 5.3-carat diamond ring in all its glory. It sparkled under the lights in the ceiling above. Immediately, I pulled it out, gazing at its brilliance when he grabbed my wrist and said, "Let me see that, let me see that." He wanted to look at the ring and was so excited that, in his mind, he was already receiving it. He explained this to me afterward because he didn't want to give me the ring after seeing how spectacular it was.

I snatched the ring back from him, slid it on my left ring finger, and said, "Yes, yes!" Finally, at forty-seven, I got the ring I always thought I deserved. He didn't say anything, nor did he ask me to marry him; he just looked at me, wondering what just happened. Without saying a word, we were engaged, and he went along with it. He seemed pleased that I was happy for the first time in our entire relationship. I don't think he realized what he was giving me at that time, and he thought, "Okay, I must have done something right," and he didn't want to ruin it for me at that time. It was the one time that I could freely express myself, showing how happy I was without him telling me to calm down.

We had been together for eighteen years at this point with an age difference of sixteen years between us. At one point during our relationship, he did put a 3-carat diamond ring on my left hand, just for show, so that I looked like I was unavailable and wouldn't be approached by other men. Now, he had given me a 5.3-carat diamond, which meant more to me than anything else he had ever done. I felt as if I had been elevated to the position of his wife. I thought of it as a promotion that I had earned… and I took it. I took it and ran with it. I was so happy. Everything he had done before that moment that was bad, everything with his kids, employees, brother, sister-in-law, ex-wife, you name it, all of it just melted away as soon as I put that ring on my finger. It was like I started with a clean slate as his fiancée.

A few days had passed, and he often grabbed my left hand to look at the diamond. He was mesmerized by what he had put on my finger. It was almost like I was a mannequin wearing his diamond, but he didn't understand that it was my diamond. He kept thinking of it as his diamond, the one he put on his prize. Like, I was an object to him that he was polishing up and making shinier. Even though I knew that, I didn't care because I was finally his fiancée, and that's all I kept thinking about.

It was December of 2019 when I received my ring, and in January of 2020, the COVID-19 pandemic exploded. While we were planning the wedding, I knew we couldn't have more than 15 people due to pandemic safety guidelines and laws. It was new to everyone, so I didn't plan a big wedding, but I wanted our relationship and my position in this bond to be celebrated.

Since my fiancé was very wealthy, I could have had anything for our wedding. We decided that we would get a beautiful cake, but he soon reminded me, or I should say corrected me, by telling me that I wasn't going to spend a lot of money on this wedding and to keep it simple. We would spend money on the cake and my dress.

"Well, can we spend money on flowers?" I asked.

"Flowers are a waste of money," he stated.

It was then that I realized it wasn't going to be celebrated the way I wanted. I had no friends during my eighteen-year relationship with him. When I became an adult entertainer, all my friends disappeared. When I started dating him, they judged me poorly, and they all left me. I kept my relationship with him extremely private, because that's what you did in that line of work. As professionals, it was a well-established rule that we couldn't expose the gentleman who were hiring us. So, I put him in a box, and I protected him.

Once he was divorced, and we were openly in a relationship, he continued wanting me to keep him private. He didn't want me to talk about him, or say who he was, or what he did. I just assumed it had something to do with his work; maybe he didn't want people to know that I was an adult entertainer before, or that was how we met. I had no idea he was putting his own story of how we met out in public. He was telling people that we had only known each other for that year, and by the time our marriage ended, he was telling people he had only known me for 5 years, even though we had been together for 22 years. He didn't want to look bad and made me look like a gold digger. Friends were telling him, "You can't marry her. You have only known her a short time. She is a gold digger." I was so pissed off when I found that out in later years. All he did was laugh at me.

Getting back to the wedding planning, I enjoy gardening, and I love flowers. If there is one thing that was important to me for the wedding, it was having beautiful flowers. After a few months of convincing, he finally agreed and allowed me to order flowers for our wedding. We ended up spending $7,000 on the flowers that turned out to be the most expensive part of our wedding. It made me cry, something I generally did not do in front of him, but I couldn't help it. I cried so badly to have flowers, though it was such a simple gesture, but after explaining to him how important flowers are to a wedding, he finally gave in.

After it is all said and done, I don't remember the flowers at our wedding. Every miserable moment in my life with him, I suppress the tiny things, so all I know is that they were burgundy. Since he made such a big deal about not ordering flowers, and I begged him for months to have them, it was like it no longer mattered to me. It took the fun out of it, something he knew how to do very well. When the flowers did arrive, we had two beautiful arches and my bouquet.

My fiancé wanted to have a long engagement, like two or three years, but I said no.

"I waited this long to get this ring. I'm getting married in a year!" I said.

"A year?" he replied.

"Yes, I'm so happy and excited to be your wife. Let's do this," I said, insisting we set a date sooner rather than later.

During my engagement, I was allowed to talk to some of my old classmates. This was something in my life that I wanted to share with them—something innocent, clean, and beautiful. I contacted four of my old friends from high school, and to my surprise, they got together and organized a bachelorette party at a hotel. It wasn't much, but I did appreciate their efforts. I had never even received a baby shower when I was pregnant, and I've never been celebrated! The fact that they put something together just for me meant the world to me.

I still didn't tell them about the drama I was dealing with my fiancé; I just wanted everything to look perfect on the outside, because that's how my fiancé had made his persona. We finally picked a date - January 29th, 2021. I wanted a winter wedding because it's too hot for me in the summer to wear a wedding gown. I can't take the heat; it would have killed me.

"I want to get married in January, because it's going to be nice and cold, and I can be a little snow princess," I said to him.

He agreed, so I told my friends that we were getting married on Saturday, the 29th, and it was going to be wonderful.

Well, the week is coming up to my wedding, when I received a call from my fiancé on Wednesday, and he said, "Hey, let's not get married on the 29th. Let's get married today. We'll go to the town office and just get married at the town office."

I said, "Wow, how romantic."

Honestly, he had never been romantic or wanted to do anything spontaneous, like, in the movies, whisking me off my feet. So, I agreed, especially since he wanted to get married sooner, rather than wait for our wedding day. I thought it was awesome. So, I went to his house with my son, and we went to the town hall. It was nothing special. He didn't dress up or wear high-end clothes, and there were no flowers. I don't generally dress up. I've always dressed very casually and comfortably, but I wore nice slacks and a warm sweater because it was winter.

When we went to the town office, we made jokes about it. He had a sense of humor when he wanted to, and it was coming out. We were having fun, and he was being playful, so I was enjoying it. I had no idea that I was getting the bare minimum.

He said, "We don't need to put all this time into a wedding when we can just go sign a piece of paper, and I can make you happy."

I never looked at it like that. I always tried to find the positive, but he was stressed out about something; I assumed it had to be work or his kids. I always respected him for his hard work because he worked 10-hour days. When we were getting married at the town office, he bought me a souvenir mug with the name of the town where we got married embossed on the front.

He said, "Here, you want a coffee cup, honey?"

I honestly said, "Sure, why not?" So, I have a coffee cup from our wedding day.

That Saturday rolled around, and because we had already bought the flowers and everything else, he said I could still celebrate by wearing my wedding gown and having my friends over to his house.

I said, "Well, why don't we have my nephew announce us as husband and wife?"

"What?" he asked.

"Yeah - he could stand where a preacher would be, and you could stand by him, and then I could walk down an aisle that we can make with my friends on each side."

"Okay," he replied, not really caring about it.

Since he wouldn't let me spend money on a photographer or someone to record the wedding, I asked the only friend of his that I was ever introduced to, and had him record the wedding. However, this gentleman was always late and irresponsible, and sure enough, he showed up late for my wedding, so there is no film or video of our little ceremony.

I have no memory of my wedding, me getting dressed, or doing my hair, none of the excitement or joy that you usually see a bride-to-be experience. There are a few pictures that one of my girlfriends took and shared with me, and I was thankful for them, but nothing like a typical wedding would have. Honestly, I didn't know that I was missing things because no one was guiding me in this endeavor. He had been a groom in two weddings already, and you would think he could have made some suggestions or helped me with the planning, but that didn't happen. He gave me a box with a ring in it, and I slid it on my hand, and then I blindly walked down the aisle.

When I saw him at the end of the aisle, I just started crying because he looked so beautiful! He looked like the perfect man, exactly what I always wanted. At the same time, I was so scared because I was crying in front of my friends. I wanted them to think they were happy tears. I put way too much thought into everything I did, because I was scared of getting in trouble. My emotions, which were normal reactions for a bride to see her groom, I got nervous about because I thought they would be misinterpreted, as they always had been. So, I ran to him and just hugged him. Nothing else was said.

I turned around and said to everyone, "Hey, you guys. We're already married! We got married this past Wednesday!"

When I made that announcement, it was like the air left the room—or a tire that had just been deflated. My friends did not look happy, and it was clear they were annoyed. I realize that a wedding is a magical time, something I was hoping to experience, but it wasn't. I felt it was taken away from me without me even seeing it happen. At that moment, I realized it wasn't being celebrated like I thought it should be. I was just being pushed along—not led—but pressed into doing something that wasn't what I had in mind.

After that announcement, we went into the dining room, and one of my friends made a speech that was quite rude, bringing up times when I wasn't in her life, things I had done wrong, and how I started my relationship with him in the most awkward way. But look how far I had come, and now I was going to be his wife. I thought to myself, "Who does that? Why was I being judged for my past at my wedding, where I thought I'd be celebrated?" I felt like I was being roasted at our wedding.

We finally sat down to a small meal in our dining room that a local restaurant catered. He sat at one end of the table, and I sat at the other, a decision I made because I liked sitting across from him so I could see him. I admired him to look at, and he liked me not being so near him, so he agreed with that. We didn't have much of a wedding party, but our friends were there on each side of the table, and while we were eating, my now-husband went upstairs and came down with a gift. I thought I was getting a wedding gift, but it wasn't. He gave my lesbian friends a bag of sex toys at the table.

He said, "I think you two will use these more than we will."

I was so embarrassed because they didn't even really know him, and here he is giving them sex toys because they were lesbians, the only lesbian couple that he pointed out. It was a very awkward moment, and dinner ended on that note. After dinner, everyone started mingling, walking around, talking, and drinking. My husband now had a couple of drinks with some friends, and they were talking, and the evening went on. By this time, it was dark out, quite early because it's winter in Maine. At 6 PM, we started playing a board game, which was the second time I had ever played one with my husband.

The first time, my son and I played a board game with him and his kids, we played Monopoly together, which turned out to be the worst game in the history of Monopoly. I didn't raise my son to cheat when playing games, but his children, including him, do so when they start losing. They cheat in any competition that they're losing. So, the Monopoly game ended poorly, and we never played another game with them.

Now it's our wedding night, and we're playing a board game for the second time. It was a board game about getting high, smoking marijuana. It was funny because I smoked a lot of marijuana, something I enjoy, and he didn't mind me doing it, because if I was high, he could get away with a lot more abuse or anything negative. After all, I would be high, so I didn't care about it, or I let it slide, and chill. As a wedding gift, one of my friends gave me a board game about smoking marijuana, and we all wanted to play it. My husband never gave me a wedding gift of any sort, but I honestly did not want to play this game with my husband. This was the first thing I felt compelled to do because I was now his wife, but I was so nervous about it.

My friends, who knew me growing up, know that I am strong-minded and don't take shit from anyone, but they had no idea about my relationship with this man of eighteen years prior, and all of the hell that he had put me through. I never told them because I didn't want them to think I was weak. And I couldn't tell him, because that was the rule in my relationship with him; I wasn't to speak about him to anyone.

So now, it felt like I was on a stage, playing this game because it was a gift. There were six or seven of us who started playing the game, and we were all having a good time, and then my husband started losing, and sure enough, cheating.

Immediately, I snapped at him and said, "You can't cheat. Stop cheating." He just looked at me and laughed, and I said again, "No, you're cheating!

My friends started saying, "There she goes. De-De's gonna go off," because they had seen it happen so many times before in high school. I did not take shit from anybody, only because I had been abused and abandoned, so I took it upon myself to be strong and not let people get away with anything that I didn't want with me involved. I was not going to be a part of their plan of attack.

I couldn't hold back, and I said, "You fucking cheat all the time."

He looked at me, shocked and baffled, and asked, "What are you talking about?"

I said, "You cheat! You cheat at every board game you fucking ever played. I fucking hate playing games with you. And this is my wedding night."

We got in a fight over him cheating in a simple board game, because the spotlight was put on me by my friends, trying to defend myself, because they have always seen me fight for myself.

He was very embarrassed when I called him out, which made him extremely angry with me. He told me the worst thing about me was my honesty, but I always thought that was a good thing. The wedding night turned out not to be much fun. It felt like I was dating him, but now I'm wearing a diamond. That night, we didn't have sex, and the next day was like a typical day. Everyone had left, and I cleaned up.

That morning, I spoke to my husband about having my dog live with us now that we were married, since he had bought me two dogs. I told him I wouldn't bring both of them, just the youngest one. The oldest dog could stay with my son at my house, where I lived before we got married.

When I told my husband I was going to get my dog, he said, "What? I didn't marry you so you could bring your dog here."

"He's my dog," I replied.

Eventually, he agreed, and I was so happy that my dog could live with me. I'm a huge pet lover. That night, I went outside on the porch to smoke some marijuana because I wasn't allowed to smoke it in the house. He lives in a state where marijuana is illegal, but I live in a state where marijuana is legal, but that didn't stop me from smoking.

While I was smoking, I had no idea that my dog was chewing on the doorframe of his house. Since my dog loved me so much, he suffered from separation anxiety, and so he was trying to get to me without me realizing it. Now, I had to tell my husband that my dog, who had only been there for less than 24 hours, had already ruined the front door frame. He got furious, called my dog a few names, and told me that he was not allowed there anymore, because he wasn't going to have his house fucking ruined by my fucking mutt.

My dog is not a mutt by any means and is a costly breed of dog, a Tibetan Mastiff. I was sad, but I understood, too. I was always reasonable. I tried to be rational with his reasoning for not allowing me to have things. He was really good at convincing me that it would be better and cause fewer problems if I just did what he suggested. Since I always respected my husband, because he always put food on my table, and fed my son. I took my dog back to my house, told my son what the dog had done, and said, "He is going to have to stay here."

"Not a problem," he said, so I went back to the house.

10

STEPFORD WIFE

My first year as his wife was perfect. I made it perfect. I became the Stepford wife that I always dreamed about being. I would shower every day, and while I wasn't big on makeup, I would make myself pretty with a little mascara and lipstick. I didn't know how to curl my hair, but I would wash it and comb it in a style that didn't look disheveled. I always wore pretty dresses. Even though I didn't know how to cook, I always made sure he had a meal by ordering out. He could afford meals from restaurants for lunch and dinner, just like I provided for his children while dating him.

That said, I was great at making breakfast, something I love to do, but that is all I can make. When it came to lunch and dinner, I couldn't prepare what he wanted, and he knew this, but he was okay with it. During our first year of marriage, I asked him if he would like to start cooking with me, because I saw on social media that newly married couples would cook together. They would take cooking classes, or go to painting classes, or do something fun together.

When I would bring this up, he would always tell me, "Well, I'm tired," or "I have something going on the next day." He always had a reason why he couldn't, and it always made sense to me. He still gave me little insults and made little comments, but they didn't seem as harsh. They almost felt playful, as if he cared about my feelings. It wasn't like the insults were gone entirely; they just weren't as harsh or as often.

One time, while getting ready for dinner, I took extra time and effort to find something nice to wear and then went downstairs, thinking I looked great and felt confident in my appearance.

We went to the restaurant, and while we were sitting there, he looked at me and said, "You look good tonight. Are you wearing makeup?"

"What?" I asked.

"Are you wearing makeup? You look pretty," he repeated.

I said, "That's not a compliment to say I look pretty and ask me if I'm wearing makeup, insinuating that I wouldn't be pretty if I didn't have makeup on."

He hurt my feelings. However, when I called him out on that, it ruined the night, but I wanted to let him know, as his wife, I thought I was allowed to say what was on my mind. I felt I had earned the right to have an opinion, share my emotions and feelings, or say no, and have a say in our sexual relationship. But I didn't.

By the time my second year of marriage had come along, I had realized that what I thought was a perfect marriage was a delusion in my head. I wanted so badly to have what I was creating in my mind, but I wasn't receiving it. One day, I made the mistake of going for a walk with a friend of his, the one friend I was allowed to hang out with. He had finally moved into town, where my husband had found him an apartment. He lived down the road from us, and since he liked to go for walks a lot for his health, being a diabetic, he knew I wanted to go for walks, too.

That day, he asked me if I'd go for a walk with him, and I said, "Absolutely! It's a beautiful day! I'll meet you at your apartment."

During our walk, he told me a story about my husband who went to get a massage from two young ladies.

He said, "One of the ladies was too rough, and he couldn't keep his erection or get off."

I stopped dead in my tracks and asked, "What?"

I fucking couldn't believe what I was hearing. It made me so angry to listen to this. I was like a loaded weapon, ready to go off, but I knew I couldn't shoot because if I fired and missed the target, I was going to be in a lot of trouble for even questioning what I had just heard.

I said, "I know my husband gets a lot of massages every Wednesday and Saturday, but I never heard of him having two girls massage him.

"Oh yeah!" he said. "Saturday, he went and got a massage in Massachusetts, where he had two young girls give him a massage.

"Two young girls?" I asked, wondering if they're professionals, or licensed masseuses, meaning, are they whores?

I was upset to hear this about my husband, and his friend looked at me and realized I was questioning him for information, but he had already said too much. I didn't bring it up to my husband until probably about a week later, but it was really weighing heavily on my soul. I had to find out if it was true or if his friend was trying to start trouble. I have had people in the past try to tell me things to start trouble, and at this point in my relationship, I question everything.

My husband and I went to lunch, like we generally did, and I asked him, "Are you gonna go get a massage today?"

He said, "Yeah, I have an appointment later at 1."

"Are you going to get a massage in town, or are you going to go to Massachusetts and get your massage from those two girls that you saw a couple of weeks ago?" I asked.

He was floored, and it was the first time I saw the devil in his face.

"What the hell are you talking about?" he asked, wanting to know how I knew what he had been doing. Without him answering anything, it was written all over his face.

I said, "Oh yeah, when I went for a walk with your friend the other day, he told me about your massage with the two girls, and how one was too rough, and you couldn't keep your erection and have an orgasm, and that you just felt like it was a waste of time and money for you."

He froze and said nothing. I knew then that it was true. When he doesn't say anything, that's when it's true. When he tries to defend himself, that's when it's true. He lied all the time. He then suggested that his friend was being a troublemaker, was interested in having sex with me, and wanted to cause problems in our marriage. I wasn't supposed to be alone with him again, because it was just inappropriate for him to be talking about that, about my husband, in that way.

I said, "Alright," knowing it was complete bullshit.

The next day, I put a tracker back on my husband's vehicle. I discovered he had gone to Massachusetts a few times and could see where he was going just by looking at the satellite app on my phone. One day, I tracked him to Marie's Hair Care. Marie's Hair Care? Is he getting a haircut? Why is he going there? I didn't want to know. I didn't want my marriage to be ruined and over already. I really wanted our marriage to work, so I ignored those signs. I ignored it every time he went to Marie's Hair Care. I made excuses for him without even asking him.

I said to myself, "Well, maybe he's getting hair products for his daughter. Maybe he's getting another touch-up from his haircut, because he's always having his hair trimmed with a nice haircut to look professional at work." One way or another, I was determined to keep our marriage together and was willing to overlook any red flags.

We never celebrated Mother's Day, Christmas, Easter, or any other holidays once we were married. He said we didn't need to celebrate Mother's Day because I wasn't his mother, and his mother had passed away. We didn't need to celebrate Easter anymore because the children weren't around—they were too old. When Christmas rolled around, I wasn't allowed to put up any decorations because he didn't like that holiday.

Once we were married, all celebrations of any kind for holidays were taken away from me. I had to celebrate them at my son's house—well, my house—where my son was living. I would put up a tree there and open gifts there. That is when I realized I was getting the bare minimum; even though I was living in a mansion, it felt more like I was living in a box.

By the end of our second year of marriage, going into our third, my three nephews, whom I was very close to and adored, came to visit me. While I was downstairs, hanging out with my nephews, we were all planning on going to dinner. So, I had to go upstairs and ask my husband about it because, after all, the decision-making was his after everything was said and done. We knew where we wanted to eat, but we still had to run it by him.

When I went upstairs, I wasn't tiptoeing or anything, and I don't weigh a lot, but I walk like a heavy elephant. I stomped my way upstairs, and by the time I got into the bedroom, I overheard my husband having a conversation with someone on the phone in the bathroom. I still had to go through his master closet to get to the bathroom. As I continued walking, I slowed my pace and didn't walk as heavily. I didn't want to run into the bathroom being rude, because it wasn't uncommon for him to be on the phone about patients or talking to his staff about important matters.

I heard my husband ask the person on the other end if the new girl was young and skinny. What the fuck did I just hear? And then a woman with an Asian accent said, "I have two new girls, both young and skinny."

He asked, "Is one of the new girls Lori? I have already seen her."
She said, "Yes."

"I want to see the other new girl," he said, so she booked him for the other new girl.

I fucking couldn't believe I had just spent two years married to him, tracking him, thinking he was going to a hair salon. Here I am, in the third year of marriage, with my nephew's downstairs, and I need to know where we're going to dinner, and this was just thrown in my fucking face.

I put on that perfect face and acted like I hadn't just heard what I'd just heard. I cleared my throat to give my husband time enough to get off the phone without him realizing that I had already listened to his conversation.

I called his name and said, "Hey, we know where we're going to go eat! Can I run it by you?"

He came right out of the bathroom, and I was standing there, but he didn't connect the dots. The look on my face wasn't anything abnormal, asking him a question, because I always had to ask him for permission. The tension was always there during our communications, and when I had to say something, he never figured that out.

We went to dinner, and while we were there, we played a video game the restaurant had on the table called Trivia Pursuit. While we were waiting for our food, my nephew sat across from us, and I had to sit by my husband. I sat inside, my husband sat outside, and the Trivia Pursuit game was closer to the outside of the table. While we were playing, we would answer the questions, and I ended up getting quite a few correct, as I was on my husband's team.

As I was answering them, he was giving the opposite answer to what I was saying, so it was coming up wrong. But at the same time, my husband's body position had turned. He had his back to me because I was having fun and excited. I had put what I heard earlier with him on the phone in the back of my mind, and now I am enjoying a simple Trivia Pursuit game and getting the answers right.

Finally, my nephew asked, "Hey, uncle. Why won't you put Auntie's answer in? She's always right, she's right."

Completely turning his back to me, he shut me out of the game completely, not allowing me even to read the next question. It was a sign of things to come. As long as my husband had his appointments, or had women lined up, I was no longer a priority. I was no longer anything. He was just on to the next affair, but he had no idea that I knew what he was doing.

Every chance I had, I would ask him for something. I would tell him that I needed money, and this was the only way I could justify what I was allowing him to do to me while we were married. So, I would ask for an outrageous amount of money.

For example, I might say, "I need $15,000 tomorrow for… whatever," and he would give it to me, most likely out of guilt, because he knew what he had just done. That is how he justified his actions and made it okay for him to do what he was doing. Without each of us knowing what we were doing, we allowed it to happen. The reason he showered me with expensive gifts and money was because of his own guilt. He told me this by saying, "Don't I give you enough for me to do what I want to do?"

11

THE MIND GAMES

From the moment we started having simple conversations as a married couple, he began manipulating my mind. I knew it would be challenging being married to him, but I didn't realize how difficult it would be. I always thought I was a great communicator and could say what was on my mind when I was allowed to express myself. Now that I was his wife, I thought I would be free to express myself, but I hadn't earned that badge yet. I still had to watch what I said to him.

One day, while we were at lunch, I said to him, "This watermelon is sour."

He looked at me with a confused look on his face and asked, "What did you just say?"

He constantly questioned what I said. For an intelligent man, he seemed pretty dumb to me, especially when I spoke clearly and in plain English.

"This watermelon tastes sour to me," I repeated.

He said, "Oh, you mean the melon. The melon tastes sour."

I said, "Are you really gonna do this right now? I'm having a good day. Why do you want to try to confuse me and make me upset?"

Again, I was now the problem in true narcissist form.

The Sandwich Incident

On another occasion, I made the mistake of asking him to do something simple for me that I knew he could do, but he would probably fuck it up somehow. I called him from my camp and told him that my friends and I were going to another football game. He seemed excited for me and asked me if there was anything he could do.

I said, "Honestly, honey, if you could just pick us up three sandwiches from the deli, that would be great."

He seemed excited that I actually needed him to do something for me, since I'd gotten used to doing things myself because I was constantly disappointed. I had faith in him this time, though. It was three simple ham-and-cheese sandwiches.

"Do you need anything else?" he asked. "Do you need sodas or chips?"

I replied, "No, we just need three sandwiches."

He asked me, "Anything on the sandwiches?"

I said, "No, honey. Simply ham and cheese. Making it as simple as possible. No mayo, mustard, oil, or vinegar. Just meat and cheese."

He was the type to constantly insist that we needed more than what we wanted. I didn't want to seem like a pig or feel guilty about not receiving, so I kept being strict about my answers. "No, honey, we simply need the sandwiches."

On my three-hour ride back to the house before the game, he called four times, asking me again, "Honey, are you sure you don't need soda and chips?"

By this time, I was annoyed. I said, "No! Please just get us ham-and-cheese sandwiches."

He felt like I was becoming unappreciative of him. By this time, I felt guilty because I didn't need the soda or chips. I'm sorry for bothering you, making you feel like I was being a total bitch. I wasn't. He was acting like a child.

When I got to the house with my friends, we got in the car we'd rented to go to the game. We usually had a driver, so we wouldn't have to worry about parking. That was another bonus I loved about being married to my husband—that he had enough money for a driver for any event I would attend. I would always take full advantage of this.

During our trip to the game, my friends and I became hungry. We opened the sandwiches—the simple ham-and-cheese—but to our surprise, they were completely smothered in mayonnaise. Knowing that I had told my husband several times we didn't want the sandwiches with mayo, oil, or mustard, and that we wanted them dry, I couldn't believe what I saw. Honestly, in the back of my head, I wasn't surprised, because I knew he wanted to find some way to ruin my day with my friends. He knew putting all that mayonnaise on my sandwiches would make me angry.

I didn't react that way, though. I let it slide.

I told my friends, "You know what? He's gonna want me to call him and bitch, but I'm not going to do that. I'm gonna enjoy my day."

My friends and I took paper towels and wiped off the sandwiches to how we preferred them. We ate them, and by the time we got to the game, my husband had called me, asking with excitement, "Honey, did I get the sandwiches right? Did I make them perfect for you?"

I said, "Absolutely, honey, they were delicious, thank you so much," knowing I was lying, and I didn't want him to get the satisfaction of annoying me and making me upset.

"Are you sure? Are you sure the sandwiches were perfect?" he asked again. He was digging. He wanted me to bitch about the mayo.

"Honey, I swear I told the guy only to put on a little mayo. Are you sure there was only a little mayo on them?" he questioned.

Acting as if I'd asked for the mayo. At that point, I didn't give a shit. I guess I was faking it until I made it.

Later that night, when I arrived home from the game, I was tired. When I saw my husband, he reminded me who had paid for the day, the ride, and the tickets. I looked at him the same way I always did—with a blank stare. Like, where is this fucking coming from? I just wanted to go upstairs and go to bed. So, I did. He constantly tried to remind me: if I had a good day, or if I was ignoring his attempts to piss me off, he would always remind me who paid for the day.

Bedtime Routine

Bedtime with my husband was a routine he came up with because he had to get up early for work, which I completely understood. This was something I had to do, even if I wasn't tired.

By the time 8 o'clock rolled around, the TV would be shut off, and I would have to lie in bed, wide awake, reading the words off my phone, so I wouldn't bother him or keep him awake.

We slept under different blankets, which was my idea. I'll admit it was kind of strange, but I chose to do this because while we were dating, we shared the same blankets. I was constantly woken up by him trying to please himself with my sleeping body. One particular night, he woke me up because he couldn't sleep and spoke to me a little bit about what was on his mind. He said he still couldn't sleep and asked me to give him a blow job.

When I told him I was tired, he replied by saying, "Don't I give you enough money to blow me any time I want a blow job?"

I got up and went to sleep on the couch. He followed me into the living room, swinging the bedroom door wide open, which caused the handle to go through the wall.

That made him mad, and he went upstairs, woke my son, and made us drive home in the middle of the night. He didn't speak to me for three days after that–eventually calling me and asking me about what I had been up to as if nothing had happened. I was never allowed to reflect on what had happened–I had to learn to choose my battles.

Looking Back on my 35th Birthday

On my 35th birthday, I was excited and looking forward to the day. I still appeared young. I felt like rainbows and unicorns. I was 35, but I looked 20. I felt like the world was mine. I believed what I was doing was right because I still looked young, vibrant, fresh, and fun.

That night, my now-husband, my boyfriend at the time, took me to a hotel where we had a few drinks. My son was allowed to come, and one of my older nephews joined us to keep my son company while we were celebrating with drinks in the lobby. Since I didn't drink a lot, and my husband was paying, I asked him, "Please don't buy me any more than two drinks. I don't want to get too drunk, because I don't want to be hungover in the morning. I have to take care of my son." Eventually, two of my girlfriends, my boss, and her friend joined us in the lobby for drinks, which he also treated them.

I'm not sure how many drinks he bought me and all of us that night, but I blacked out. I knew I threw up sometime earlier in the evening, because I remember seeing it in the toilet bowl in the bathroom with my girlfriends. I don't remember anything after that, other than waking up with my legs over my head and my boyfriend having sex with me. I was utterly stunned by his actions. He obviously knew I was passed out and drunk, but he had sex with me anyway, without my knowledge, until I came to with my legs over my head, something that I never did knowingly. I just shut my eyes with shame and let him continue what he had to do. I passed back out and woke up the next morning.

I looked at him with disgust in my eyes when I saw him and said, "You date-raped me last night."

He laughed and said, "Honey, I'm your boyfriend. I can't rape you."

"That's why it's called date rape, asshole. I know you, and you know me. And you had sex with me while I was passed out. I didn't even know what was going on until I woke up with my legs over my head," I explained.

He said, "Don't worry, honey, you enjoyed it."

I couldn't believe what he said. I never hated him any more than at that moment.

As his wife, my first rule in the marital bed was to get my own blanket so I would have a peaceful night's sleep. He agreed with it because I explained why. If my husband wanted to know whether I was still in bed the next morning, he wouldn't reach over gently to wake me or even say my name. He would just slap his hand down on my blankets, aggressively.

When I would get irritated with this—because he was abruptly waking me up out of a dead sleep—it would come across that I was being a bitch.

He would wake me up and ask me, "Oh, what, did you wake up on the wrong side of the bed?"

I would explain to him, "I just woke up by you slapping me."

There it is. Again, he ruined my morning.

It was constant—any situation that became simple, I made simple, hoping it wouldn't become complicated. But even the simplest tasks became a problem, where I was confused what my next move would be. I was consistently playing out scenarios in my head for the simplest situations—the pros and cons, what would happen if I said or did that—while at the same time getting my point across without looking like a pig, a term he often called me.

12

THE RING THAT CHANGED NOTHING

The Price of a Puppy

Within the first year I was with my boyfriend, I got pregnant with his child, and I had to end the pregnancy. My first pregnancy was the miscarriage that I spoke about in an earlier chapter. My second pregnancy was my son. A year after my son was born, his father and I were intimate, and I got pregnant with his child. I told him I didn't want this child because he was not a good dad to his children. Why would I bring a second child into this world? So, I had to make the most difficult decision a woman has to make. I ended the pregnancy.

My fourth pregnancy came when my son was three, and I had known my boyfriend, now husband, for a year. He had bought me a house closer to his house when I found out I was pregnant with his child. I knew it was his because I had not been with anyone else. I've never been disloyal to him and have always been faithful.

He convinced me, because he was still married with two children, that it wouldn't work, and I should terminate the pregnancy. If I had followed through with what he wanted me to do, he would have gotten me the puppy I wanted earlier in our relationship. And so, I stopped the pregnancy.

He came to visit me the day the procedure was done. I did write in the medical documents that I did know who the father was, because I wasn't going to be ashamed of that, and I did write his full name, which took place in Portland, Maine. Later that day, he came to the house he had purchased for my son and me. I thought he was there to check on me, to see how I was doing—my well-being, my health, my mental state, because I just had a major traumatic procedure done to my body. And that takes a toll on a female, even if it is her third or fourth pregnancy. He came over just to see if I had done it, to make sure I wasn't lying, to make sure the abortion was done.

When I realized that, I got pissed. And he was trying to shame me. He said, "I don't even know if it's mine. I'm a married man," making it as if I got myself pregnant, because how could a married man get me pregnant? Remember, he was still married to his second wife at this point.

And we argued, and he called me a whore. While he was leaving, I threw an apple pie at his car, and I don't know how he explained that to his wife when he arrived home. Maybe he went to the car wash before, but there was apple pie all over the front of his car. And that was the end of that. We never discussed the pregnancy again. And I got my dog a month later.

Chicago and False Hopes

One day, he surprised me with a trip to Chicago, one of my favorite cities. I love the hot dogs and how they put a pickle on them. They're delicious. While walking around downtown, I had a hot dog, and we ended up going to a jewelry store. It wasn't uncommon for us to pop into a jewelry store so he could look at the watches and other shiny, expensive things. But this time, it was different. He was asking me what I thought, what I liked. While that may sound wonderful, it also triggered an unpleasant flashback to a time years ago, when we were dating, when he asked me to bring a t-shirt on vacation that said "Girlfriend to Fiancé" that I had found at Goodwill.

We were on our way to Florida, and I brought the T-shirt so I could wear it. I was thinking, wow, girlfriend-to-fiancé—this must mean I'm getting engaged. I'm gonna be proposed to on our Florida trip this time. But that wasn't true.

While I was wearing the shirt, he said, "You look silly wearing that shirt."

"Silly. You're the one who told me to bring it," I replied.

"Yeah, I didn't expect you to wear it," he said with a scoff.

I was so embarrassed and said, "I'm wearing it because I thought you were going to propose to me."

"Propose to you? Why on earth would I do that?" he asked. I was humiliated. I actually believed that he was going to marry me.

Remembering this, now we were in Chicago looking for diamonds. I really didn't hope anything would come out of it at all, but I didn't want to ask any questions. When he would ask me about a ring, I would say, "Yeah, I like that ring," or "Yeah, that's pretty." Just simple answers to his questions about the diamonds. There was one ring that really stood out to me—a gorgeous 5.3 carat diamond solitaire that the jeweler sized for my finger. No explanation was given and we simply left the store.

Unknowingly, while in Chicago, he purchased the ring that I picked out and surprised me with it in December of 2019. I was floored. I was the happiest girl in the world. Everything he had done to me prior, everything that his kids had said to me and did to me was gone. It was immediately erased by this shiny diamond that I had in my hand. I felt like I had finally won the prize. However, what I received was not a prize at all.

The Non-Proposal

There was no proposal. He never actually asked me to marry him. The ring had arrived at his office, and he came home with it, looking very excited about something. I had no idea what he was excited about. He said, "I have something for you."

It could have been a new handbag or a new outfit. He loved buying me Louis Vuitton clothing, so it could have been anything. I wasn't expecting a diamond. We went upstairs into his bedroom, and he sat down on the edge of the bed and said, "Here, sit down, I want to show you something. I want to give you something." In anticipation of what he had for me; I was very excited because I'd never seen him so animated and enthusiastic. With a dry personality, he never showed excitement for much of anything.

A red box appeared, and he gently laid it in my hand. I unwrapped it, lifted the front end of the box, and there sat the 5.3-carat diamond ring in all its glory. It sparkled under the lights in the ceiling above. Immediately, I pulled it out, gazing at its brilliance when he grabbed my wrist and said, "Let me see that, let me see that."

He wanted to look at the ring and was so excited that in his mind, he was already receiving it. He explained this to me afterward because he didn't want to give me the ring after seeing how spectacular it was.

I snatched the ring back from him, slid it on my left ring finger, and said, "Yes!" He didn't say anything. Nor did he ask me to marry him. He just looked at me, wondering what just happened. Without saying a word, we were engaged, and he went along with it. He seemed pleased that I was happy for the first time in our entire relationship. I don't think he realized what he was giving me at that time, and he thought he must have done something right, and he didn't want to ruin it for me at that moment. It was the only time that I could freely express myself, showing how happy I was, without him telling me to calm down.

We had been together for 18 years at this point. I was 47 and he was 63. At one point during our relationship, he did put a 3-carat diamond ring on my left hand, just for show, so that it looked like I was unavailable and wouldn't be approached by other men. Now he had given me a 5.3-carat diamond, which meant more to me than anything else he'd ever done. I felt like I was elevated to the position of being his wife. I thought of it as a promotion that I had earned, and I took it. I took it and ran with it. I was so happy.

Everything he had done before that moment that was bad, everything with his kids, employees, brother, sister-in-law, ex-wife, you name it, all of it just melted away as soon as I put that ring on my finger. It was like I started with a clean slate as his fiancé.

A few days passed, and he often grabbed my left hand to look at the diamond. He was mesmerized by what he had put on my finger. It was almost like I was a mannequin wearing his diamond, but he didn't understand that it was my diamond. I had to tell him that all the time, but he kept thinking of it as a diamond that he put on his prize, like I was an object to him that he was polishing up and making shinier. Even though I knew that, I didn't care, because I was finally his fiancé. And that's all I kept thinking about.

Planning the Bare Minimum

It was December 2019 when I received my ring, and in January 2020, the COVID-19 pandemic erupted. While we were planning the wedding, I knew we couldn't have more than 15 people due to pandemic safety guidelines and laws. It was a new experience for everyone dealing with the pandemic, so I didn't plan a big wedding, but I wanted our relationship and my role in this bond to be celebrated.

Since my fiancé was very wealthy, I could have had anything for our wedding. We decided to get a beautiful cake. But he soon reminded me—or I should say corrected me—by telling me that I wasn't going to spend a lot of money on this wedding and to keep it simple. We would spend money on the cake and my dress.

"Well, can't we spend money on flowers?" I asked.

"Flowers are a waste of money," he stated. It was then that I realized it wasn't going to be celebrated the way I wanted.

I had no friends during my 18-year relationship with him. When I became an adult entertainer, all my friends disappeared. When I started dating him, they judged me poorly, and they all left me. I kept my relationship with him extremely private, because that's what you did in that line of work. As professionals, it was well established that we couldn't expose the gentlemen who hired us. So, I put him in a box, and I protected him.

Once he was divorced, and we were openly in a relationship, he continued wanting me to keep him private. He didn't want me to talk about him, or say who he was, or what he did. I just assumed it had something to do with his work. Maybe he didn't want people to know that I was an adult entertainer before, or that was how we met. I had no idea that he was putting out in the public his own story of how we met.

He was telling people that we had only known each other for that year. By the time our marriage ended, he was claiming he only knew me for five years. But in reality, we were together for 22. So, he was spreading this story to protect his reputation because he was showing off his 24-year-old girlfriend around town, and then he got back with me. He didn't want to look bad, so he crafted his own version, saying he had just met me and tried to make it seem like I was only a gold digger. All of his friends were giving him advice: "Oh, you can't marry her, you've only known her a year." Without telling them he'd been with me 18 years before, making me look like just a gold digger, I was so pissed off when I found out. He just laughed at me.

Getting back to the wedding planning, I enjoy gardening, and I love flowers. If there's one thing that was important to me for the wedding, it was having beautiful flowers. After a few months of convincing, he finally agreed and allowed me to order flowers for our wedding. We ended up spending $7,000 on the flowers that turned out to be the most expensive part of our wedding. It made me cry, something I generally did not do in front of him, but I couldn't help it. I cried so badly to have flowers, though it was such a simple gesture. But after explaining to him how important flowers are to a wedding, he finally gave in.

After it is all said and done, I don't remember the flowers at our wedding. Every miserable moment in my life with him, I suppressed the tiny things, so all I know is that they were burgundy. Since he made such a big deal about not ordering flowers, and I begged him for months to have them, it was like it no longer mattered to me. It took the fun out of it, something he knew how to do very well. When the flowers did arrive, we had two beautiful arches and my bouquet.

My fiancé wanted to have a long engagement, like two or three years, but I said no. "I waited this long to get this ring. I'm getting married in a year," I said.

"A year?" he replied.

"Yes, I'm so happy and excited to be your wife. Let's do this," I said, insisting we set a date sooner rather than later.

During my engagement, I was allowed to talk to some of my old classmates. This was something in my life that I wanted to share with them—something innocent, clean, and beautiful. I contacted four of my old friends from high school, and to my surprise, they got together and organized a bachelorette party at a hotel. It wasn't much, but I did appreciate their efforts. I had never even received a baby shower when I was pregnant, and I've never been celebrated. The fact that they put something together just for me meant the world to me. I still didn't tell them about the drama I was dealing with my fiancé. I just wanted everything to appear perfect on the outside because that's the image my fiancé had created for himself.

The Wedding That Wasn't

We finally picked a date: January 29th, 2021. I wanted a winter wedding because it's too hot for me to wear a wedding gown in the summer. I can't take the heat; it would have killed me.

"I want to get married in January, because it's gonna be nice and cold, and I can be a little snow princess," I said to him. He agreed, so I told my friends that we were getting married on Saturday the 29th, and it was gonna be wonderful.

Well, the week coming up to my wedding, I received a call from my fiancé on Wednesday, and he said, "Hey, let's not get married on the 29th, let's get married today. We'll go to the town office and just get married at the town office."

I said, "Wow, how romantic."

Honestly, he had never been romantic or wanted to do anything spontaneous, like in the movies, whisking me off my feet. I agreed, especially since he wanted to get married sooner, rather than wait for our wedding day. I thought it was awesome. So, I went to his house with my son, and we went to our local town hall.

It was nothing special. He didn't dress up or wear high-end clothes, and there were no flowers. I don't generally dress up. I've always dressed very casually and comfortably, but I wore nice slacks and a warm sweater because it was winter. When we went to the town office, we made jokes about it. He had a sense of humor when he wanted to, and it was coming out. We were having fun, and he was being playful. So I was enjoying it. I had no idea that I was getting the bare minimum. He said, "We don't need to put all this time into a wedding when we can just go sign a piece of paper and I can make you happy."

I never looked at it like that. I always tried to find the positive, but he was stressed out about something. I assumed it had to be work or his kids. I always respected him for his hard work because he worked 10-hour days. When we were getting married at the town office, he bought me a souvenir mug with the name of the town where we got married in New Hampshire on the front.

He said, "Here, you want a coffee cup, honey?"

I honestly said, "Sure, why not?" So, I have a coffee cup from our wedding day, and that was the only wedding gift I received.

That Saturday rolled around, and because we had already bought the flowers and everything else, he said I could still celebrate by wearing my wedding gown and having my friends over to his house.

I said, "Well, why don't we have my nephew announce us as husband and wife?"

"What?" he asked.

"He could stand where a preacher would be, and you could stand by him, and then I could walk down an aisle that we make with my friends on each side."

"Okay," he replied, not really caring about it.

Since he wouldn't let me spend money on a photographer or someone to record the wedding, I asked the only friend of his I had ever been introduced to to record it. However, this gentleman was always late and irresponsible, and sure enough, he showed up late for my wedding, so there is no film or video of our little ceremony.

I have no memory of my wedding, of me getting dressed or doing my hair, or of the excitement or joy you usually see a bride-to-be experience. There are a few pictures that one of my girlfriends took and shared with me, and I was thankful for them, but nothing like a typical wedding would have.

Honestly, I didn't know that I was missing things because no one was guiding me in this endeavor. He had been a groom in two weddings already, and you would think he would have made some suggestions or helped me in some way with the planning of our wedding, but that didn't happen.

He gave me a box with a ring in it, and I slid it on my hand, and then I blindly walked down the aisle. When I saw him at the end of the aisle, I just started crying, because he looked so beautiful. He looked like the perfect man, exactly what I always wanted.

At the same time, I was so scared because I was crying in front of my friends. I wanted them to think that they were happy tears. I put way too much thought into everything I did because I was scared of getting in trouble. My emotions, which were normal reactions for a bride to see her groom, I got nervous about because I thought they would be misinterpreted, as they always have been. So I ran to him and just hugged him. Nothing else was said.

I turned around and said to everyone, "Hey, you guys, we're already married. We got married this past Wednesday."

When I made that announcement, it was like the air left the room—or a tire that had just been deflated. My friends did not look happy, and it was clear that they were annoyed.

I realized that a wedding is a magical time, something I was hoping to experience, but it wasn't. I felt it was taken away from me before I even saw it happen. I realized it wasn't being celebrated the way I thought it should be. I was just being pushed along—not led, but forced— into doing something that wasn't what I had in mind.

Roasted at My Own Wedding

After that announcement, we went into the dining room. One of my friends made a speech that was quite rude, bringing up times when I wasn't in her life, things I had done wrong, and how I started my relationship with him in the most awkward way. But look how far I had come, and now I was going to be his wife. I thought to myself, who does that? Why was I being judged for my past at our wedding, where I thought I would be celebrated? I felt like I was being roasted at our wedding.

We finally sat down to a small meal in our dining room that a local restaurant catered. He sat at one end of the table, and I sat at the other, a decision I made because I liked sitting across from him so I could see him. I admired him from a distance, and he wanted me not being so near to him, so he agreed with that. Why? He enjoyed appearing single. When he felt threatened by another man, that was the only time he would hold my hand. When he would do that, I would always look around and see a man looking at me. It was never out of affection, but more about showing ownership of me.

We didn't have much of a wedding party, but our friends were there on each side of the table, and while we were eating, my now-husband went upstairs and came down with a gift. I thought I was getting a wedding gift, but it wasn't. He gave my lesbian friends a bag of sex toys at the table. He said, "I think you two will use these more than we will." I was so embarrassed, because they didn't even really know him, and here he is giving them sex toys because they were lesbians—the only lesbian couple that he pointed out. It was a very awkward moment, and dinner ended on that note.

After dinner, everyone started mingling, walking around, talking, and drinking. My husband now had a couple of drinks with some friends, and they were chatting as the evening went on. By this time, it was dark out, which was quite early because it's winter in Maine. At 6pm, we started playing a board game, which was the second time I'd ever played one with my husband.

The first time my son and I played a board game with him and his kids, we played Monopoly together, which turned out to be the worst game in the history of Monopoly. I didn't raise my son to cheat when playing games, but his children, including him, do so when they start losing. They cheat in any competition that they're losing. So, the Monopoly game ended poorly, and we never played another game with them.

Now it's our wedding night, and we're playing a board game for the second time. It was a board game about getting high, smoking marijuana. It was funny, because I smoked a lot of marijuana, something I enjoy, and he didn't mind me doing it, because if I was high, he could get away with a lot more abuse or anything negative toward me. After all, I'd be high, so I didn't care about it, or I'd let it slide and chill.

As a wedding gift, one of my friends gave me a board game about smoking marijuana, and we all wanted to play it. My husband never gave me a wedding gift of any sort, but I did not want to play this game with my husband. I was like, this is gonna be the first thing as a wife that I'm gonna have to do that I don't want to do. But I did it because I was his wife, and it was simply playing a board game, but I don't think I'd ever been so nervous.

My friends who knew me growing up know that I'm strong-minded and don't take shit from anyone, but they had no idea about my relationship with this man of 18 years prior, and all of the hell that he had put me through. I never told them, because I didn't want them to think I was weak, and I couldn't tell them, because that was the rule in my relationship with him. I wasn't to speak about him to anyone. So now, it felt like I was on a stage playing this game because it was a gift.

There were six or seven of us who started playing the game, and we were all having a good time, and then my husband started losing, and sure enough, cheating. Immediately, I snapped at him and said, "You can't cheat! Stop cheating!"

He just looked at me and laughed. And I again said, "No, you're cheating!"

My friends started saying, "There she goes, De-De's gonna go off," because they'd seen it happen so many times before in high school. I did not take shit from anybody only because I'd been abused and abandoned, so I took it upon myself to be strong and not let people get away with anything that I didn't want to get involved. I was not going to be part of their plan of attack.

I couldn't hold back, and I said, "You fucking cheat all the time."

He was shocked and baffled and asked, "What are you talking about?"

"You cheat! You cheat at every board game you have ever played. I hate playing games with you, and this is my wedding night," I said, sad and angry at the same time.

We got in a fight over him cheating in a simple board game because the spotlight was put on me by my friends, trying to defend myself because they've always seen me fight for myself. He was very embarrassed that I called him out, which made him extremely angry with me. He told me the worst thing about me was my honesty, but I always thought that was a good thing.

Our wedding night turned out not to be so much fun. It felt like I was dating him, but now I'm wearing a diamond. That night, we didn't have sex, and the next day was like a typical day. Everyone had left, and I cleaned up.

My Dog Wasn't Welcome

That morning, I talked to my husband about having my dog come live with us now that we were married. Since he had bought me two dogs, I told him I wouldn't bring both of them, only the youngest one. The oldest dog could stay with my son at my house, where I lived before we got married.

When I told my husband I was going to get my dog, he said, "What? I didn't marry you so you could bring your dog here."

"He's my dog," I replied.

Eventually, he agreed, and I was so happy that my dog could come live with me, as I am a huge pet lover. That night, I went outside on the porch to smoke some marijuana because I wasn't allowed to smoke it in the house. He lives in a state where marijuana is illegal, but I have always lived in a state where marijuana is legal, and that didn't stop me from smoking.

While I was smoking, I had no idea that my dog was chewing on the doorframe of his house. Since my dog loved me so much, he suffered from separation anxiety, and so he was trying to get to me without me realizing it. Now I had to tell my husband that my dog, who had only been there for less than 24 hours, had already ruined the front door frame.

He got furious, calling my dog a few choice names, and told me he wasn't allowed there anymore because he wasn't gonna have his house ruined by my mutt. First of all, my dog is not a mutt, by any means, and is a costly breed of dog—a Tibetan Mastiff, which my husband gladly purchased. He cost eight grand, and we flew him in from China. He even has his own passport, far from being a mutt!

I was sad, but I understood too. I was always reasonable. I tried to be rational with his reasoning for not allowing me to have things. He was really good at convincing me that it was going to be better and fewer problems if I did what he suggested. Since I always respected my husband for putting food on my table and feeding my son, I took my dog back to my house, told my son what the dog had done, and said he was gonna have to stay here. "Not a problem," he said, so I went back to the house.

The Box I Lived In

We never celebrated Mother's Day, Christmas, Easter, or any other holidays once we were married. He said we didn't need to celebrate Mother's Day because I wasn't his mother, and his mother had passed away. We didn't need to celebrate Easter anymore because the children weren't around—they were too old. When Christmas rolled around, I wasn't allowed to put up any decorations because he didn't like that holiday. Although we never celebrated the holidays together, he was still celebrating them with his kids and ex-wife.

Once we were married, all celebrations of any kind for holidays were taken away from me. I had to celebrate them at my son's house—well, my house, where my son was living. I would put up a tree there and open gifts there. That is when I realized I was getting the bare minimum, even though I was living in a mansion, but it felt more like I was living in a box.

On Easter, I found on the Ring camera that he celebrated the holiday with his children and his ex-wife, giving her a full tour of my personal space, more specifically, my closets and personal bathroom, where she commented on how spoiled I was, and I didn't appreciate it. My husband never started the conversation poorly about me but he always would agree with what was being said poorly about me on the ring camera. He never defended me.

13

THE SON'S THREATS AND ESCALATING CONTROL

One day, while my husband and I were hanging out by the pool, his son kept asking him for money. It wasn't unusual for the son to ask for cash, and he was common to text his father hundreds of times. I didn't know if he had it on speed dial or if he just had to do it manually, but he received hundreds of texts. If his father didn't respond immediately, he would start threatening him by saying things like, "I'm gonna call your wife a whore, I'm gonna email her some more things." He would insult my appearance every chance he got.

This morning, when his son asked him for money, I told him, "Why don't you just simply tell him no?"

"I wish it was that easy, honey. But my son won't stop. There's something mentally wrong with him," his father replied.

His son continued texting: "I want money now, Dad. I know you can afford it. You can afford your whore."

He then texted his father over 200 times: "I'm gonna kill your wife and blame it on you."

My husband showed me the texts where I took a screenshot of them and sent them to my phone. Then I called the police in town. I expressed my concern because his son had assaulted his mother and sister in previous situations where he didn't get his way. I felt threatened. His father knew that his son was diagnosed as a sociopath and showed some concerns with my well-being. He allowed me to contact the police, and so I did. Of course, I asked for permission first. I didn't want to upset my husband.

I knew the boy lived in Florida, but I didn't have a residential address. So, all I could show the police were the text messages his father received and that he lived in Florida. The officer said he would try his best. Fortunately, he knew my husband's son because they had gone to school together. They graduated together, and he felt bad for me because he knew, in a way, what I was dealing with—he had to deal with it in high school. He could totally relate to being around my step-son.

The Court Case

The case finally went to court. I asked my husband if he would accompany me so I wouldn't have to go alone. My husband came up with some excuse that didn't make sense to me at the time— which they never really did, but I had to take his answer for what it was. While in court, the judge told me that it made no sense to her to charge his son with any criminal activity, because he didn't text my phone; he texted his father. And if his father had come in and represented me and showed the judge his phone, then the judge would have protected me and had some grounds to charge his son with criminal threatening.

Because my husband chose to protect his son over me, I didn't get any help that day.

I called my husband once I left the courthouse, though I felt like walking home. When he picked me up and asked me how the case went, I told him it got thrown out.

He laughed and said, "Do you know the judge? She is one of my patients."

I knew I was screwed. Again, the day was ruined.

Later, I found out that my ex-husband was in court as I write this book, trying to get guardianship over his son to put him into a 90-day mental health program because he has become unsafe for being in the public and himself. He recently was arrested for firing a gun in a small group of people in Florida. They held him for three days, where he was supposed to turn himself in to the mental facility for further evaluation, but he never showed up. That is why his father had to go to court.

Communication Confusion

As his wife, I knew it would come with some challenges, but I didn't realize I would face communication challenges. I considered myself very good at expressing myself with words. Apparently, I didn't know exactly how to express myself to him.

When he wanted me to do something, he wouldn't just come out and ask me, knowing I would do it because I always did everything he asked. I was more than capable of handling it. He would start the conversation by saying, "We need to start doing this." Since he used the word "we," I assumed he included himself in the mission he proposed to me. I was wrong.

I would be told I had an attitude because I was waiting for him to help me. Usually, if he wanted me to do something, he would just ask me to do it. But if there were things he thought he should help me with—things that a husband would normally help his wife with—he would start the conversation with "we," confusing me, knowing he just wanted me to do it. I was left speechless every time he spoke to me–I would call it "Dr. Seussing" me, meaning making it a riddle.

"Why can't you just say it? Why is everything a word problem?" So I would always say to him, "Stop Dr. Seussing me."

My 50th Birthday Party

During my marriage, my husband realized my attitude, that's what he called it, was different when my friends were around. I stood up for myself. I was a little bossy, but I was productive and fun. He didn't like that side of me. I would experience the silent treatment from my husband after visiting my friends.

For my 50th birthday, I had to ask my husband if we could celebrate it with a big party, because it was a milestone for most people. I had to ask him for permission, because we never celebrated birthdays with a party. And not that I'm complaining, because going to dinner and getting gifts were simple and fun, and I enjoyed them with him. But this year, I wanted a big party.

I asked him several times, and he finally said yes. Although my birthday was in July, he made me celebrate it in September. He made it so his family would come to visit, and they hadn't visited in years. With that explanation, I was just so happy that he was allowing me to have a party, no matter what time of year.

I looked forward to this party because I was gonna make it all about me. The other parties I had were basically parties for my friends. Like Christmas, I would spoil them and get them gifts that I knew they couldn't afford on their own. I wanted to share a little bit of what I had with them during the holidays.

Back to my 50th birthday party. I celebrated it with my son and my nephews. Although my husband was caught in the wine cellar with his friend and a female band member whom he had hired to entertain us during my party, I didn't let it ruin my evening. He has been caught with his hand in the cookie jar before, so I knew he was trying to ruin it for me. That wasn't uncommon for my husband to wander off, as my son would put it.

I don't drink alcohol. I mainly smoke marijuana. But today, I was gonna have a drink. It would loosen me up a little bit, so I didn't care about anyone's opinion of me. I was going to enjoy myself. That was probably the worst thing I could have done. The next day, my husband got up without letting any of us know. He went outside to start cleaning up after the fun event. He didn't realize that my friends and I, and nephews who had spent the night, were planning on cleaning up after we had smoked a blunt upstairs on the third floor, something my husband allowed me to do. Occasionally, my husband would join me in smoking marijuana, which allowed me to smoke inside now that he was doing it too.

To our surprise, my husband was outside dragging a black garbage bag around the yard, picking up trash and bottles. We shared a few words about his cleaning up.

"Why aren't you all helping?" he asked.

I explained to him that we were on our way out to clean up, but he had beaten us to it. He walked inside without saying another word to me for the next four days. The days had passed, and I realized I was getting the silent treatment longer than usual. I didn't have a therapist or anyone at this time I could talk to. However, I learned to trust this one woman whom I met while I picked up my medication once a month. When I picked up my prescription, I would basically trauma dump on her and tell her all about the situations at home with my husband.

I would give her examples of the unexplainable situations I was dealing with. Usually, there were conversations about how he would try to trick my mind and make me think that what I was saying was wrong. Then he would try to get me to say what he wanted me to say, but I wouldn't.

This was getting confusing to me. She explained to me that he might be a narcissist. I'd never heard that term before. She explained to me what a narcissist was, and I agreed with her.

I went home later that night and explained to my husband, "I think you're a narcissist."

He took it as a compliment and said, "Thank you."

I quickly explained to him that it wasn't a complement, and he gave me a dirty look.

The Friend Who Wasn't

My friends weren't allowed to stop by whenever they wanted. I'd have to ask my husband first for permission if they could come and visit me. If he had granted me permission, they would have come and spent the whole weekend, because the drive was long, and I hated for them to have to just come and quickly leave.

My husband and one of my friends, without my knowledge, would wander off together and do shots of alcohol and take selfies together. She would post them on her Snapchat, knowing that I didn't know how to look them up. She wasn't a friend that I could trust any longer I found out through my son. My son would watch my husband and her wander off together, while my other friends and I were out looking at my prizes that my husband had bought me.

My son would say, "Mom, you would go, 'Hey, friends, let's go upstairs so I can show you what I just got,' and act so happy, and act like your husband was spoiling you. Your friends would follow you up with excitement, but that one friend, the one who sold insurance, would tag along in the back. And your husband would come up behind her and slap her on the ass, and they would slide into the closet and start giggling. Your friend isn't a friend." My son always says it how it is.

I had mentioned this to her, and she denied it. During our conversation about what I was accusing her of, she explained to me that she didn't know how she made good choices in her life, and I had made bad choices. Her opinion of me being a stripper—but her life wasn't as glamorous as mine. She said she didn't think I deserved my life, and that she deserved it. She compared herself to another one of our friends who also sells insurance. She reminded me of the girl in the movie "Single White Female," who secretly wanted my life—and it showed. She was jealous of us.

"The other insurance lady and I could buy whatever we wanted without question," she said.

I had no idea how much that bothered her, and that she was after my life and my husband. I wanted to give her the benefit of the doubt, because I had known her since I was four. She did confide in me that she had not been intimate with her husband for the past seven years, making it shocking to me that she was so flirtatious toward my husband.

The Christmas Kiss

Last Christmas, I finally saw her true colors. My husband got extremely drunk, blaming my friends for being late or not attending due to weather conditions. I'd never seen my husband this drunk before. He was falling over couches, behaving in a way I'd never witnessed.

Sometime during the evening, while we were all dancing on a makeshift dance floor, my husband started approaching me, and I was getting ready to walk into his arms.

To my surprise, he walked right by me. He wasn't walking towards me, he was walking towards my friend. They started kissing. I couldn't believe my eyes. They were kissing right in front of everyone, and not for a moment, like a peck on the lips as a joke, but like they were making out in front of everyone.

When I realized they weren't gonna stop, and this wasn't a joke, I pulled my husband away from my friend, pushing him onto the floor. This was the same woman.

My friend approached me with a massive grin on her face and said, "Don't worry, De-De, we didn't use tongue."

My husband got back to his feet, laughed in my face, and said, "Yes, we did."

I never trusted her after that, knowing she was just a little thirsty bitch. The next day, my husband denied everything, not realizing that he had done it right in front of the whole Christmas party. Once I explained that to him—that everyone witnessed it—he admitted to it, and said he did it because he was drunk. He reassured me that she wasn't his type, and we went on our day, and I accepted that he was just drunk. I no longer hung out with that friend because I couldn't trust her.

The Daily Lists

He would give thoughtful gifts. I loved his presents. I still loved him deep inside, and I wanted him to know I appreciated his hard work, so I would always try to stay productive for him. He would have a list for me every day, and he would go through it each morning before he left for work. I completed everything on that list, because if I didn't complete one thing for any reason, I would be belittled and shamed. I had to move a 30-foot carpet rolled up in a U-Haul, and I pulled my back out one day, and he got mad at me because once I pulled my back out, I couldn't carry it in the house. He was furious at me for hurting myself, and I would not be able to do much of anything the next day, certainly not complete another to-do list.

The Vacation Lies

While we were married, our vacations became fewer, although he still traveled alone. He explained that he needed breaks, his back hurt, and he needed to refuel. I wanted to be understanding and just go along with it. I found out, with his permission, of course, by looking at his phone to see photos of my son and me from a previous vacation. I noticed there were pictures on his phone of him and his daughter while he was on vacation.

It only made sense to me that he was meeting his daughter while he was going on vacation alone. I immediately asked him, "Are you meeting up with your daughter in Florida while you're telling me that you need to do this alone?"

He got mad at me, grabbed his phone, and said, "What are you doing? Snooping?"

"No, I'm simply looking up photos, and this picture of you and your daughter came up. Who took the photo?" I asked him.

He said, with a grin, "It was one of her friends."

I confronted him. "I don't think it's appropriate that you're going on vacation with your daughter and her 20-year-old friends while you're telling me that you're going alone, feeling like I'm the good wife, giving you something you need, but you're lying to me! And now I'm the bad person, because you're lying to me."

He made it all about me being a snoop, and now he can't go on vacation to visit his daughter. It wasn't that at all. It was that he was lying. Why did he have to lie about meeting up with his daughter if that was simply all he was doing? I would have understood. It was basically another headache for me to find out that he was lying about another simple task that he performed on a daily basis.

You would think he would be exhausted with all the lying.

The Weight Control

It wasn't uncommon for me to see my husband flirt with other women. After a few years of being married, at the age of 50, I thought for my health, I should put on at least 10 pounds. I wasn't allowed to put on weight. I was told to stay 103, and that's where I stayed. I didn't ask my husband if I could gain some weight, so I just started secretly eating because he would monitor what was in the refrigerator. He would always ask me while he held the refrigerator door open, "What's this in here? Are you going to eat this? Who is this for?"

I would respond by nervously telling him it was me and had to reassure him that I was not going to eat it all. "I'm just going to eat a little," I said to reinforce my argument. He was constantly worried about me putting on weight. He would often mention that his ex-wife put on weight during their marriage, which led to their divorce. I took that as a threat, to be honest.

I would stop at a gas station right before the highway and grab a slice of pizza. I thought, what better way to put weight on than to sit on my ass and eat a slice of pizza? It worked. I put on the weight, and I felt comfortable and confident, something I had never felt about my body with weight on. I always knew I'd be punished for being told to go home to lose the weight if I had mentioned anything about gaining weight. So, keeping it a secret, I had to wear baggy clothes.

When my husband realized my ass was bigger—a gentleman that he had met had mentioned, "Your wife has a nice ass." Of course he didn't appreciate the comment, but it also made my husband realize I was getting bigger.

My husband explained to me that he didn't like my big ass, and I was to go home to lose the weight. He bought me my second elliptical, and this time, I also got a rower, because he wasn't happy with my legs. They were just simply aging. I wasn't as toned as I was when I was younger. I had developed some cellulite, even as a thin person, on my thighs.

I explained to him that I kept trying to remove the cellulite with exercise, creams, and lotions, but he explained to me that it wasn't working. He didn't like my excuses for having cellulite on my legs.

He told me, "I'll make a deal with you. I'll take you to Paris if you get the cellulite off your legs and make them look like when you were 20." I didn't care too much about going to Paris. What bothered me was that he was making comments about my legs, and I only weighed 103.

Paris was the place where my husband would take his side chicks on vacations when he wanted to spoil them. I found this out during a trip he had taken one of his girlfriends on the week of my birthday. His flight was delayed in New York, and he had to drive home by renting a car.

On my birthday, that night, we had dinner, and he didn't explain anything to me. I found this out from one of his friends that I wasn't allowed to have contact with, but his friend was secretly attracted to me, and he thought if he had approached me with this information, I would leave my husband and go with him, as if he was my knight in shining armor.

I told this gentleman, "I'm still loyal to my husband."

This gentleman replied, "Even after all I've told you?"

I said, "Yes," and my son asked him to leave.

They were flying back from Paris and were supposed to land in Boston that morning, which was my birthday. Because the flight from New York was delayed, their return flight was delayed as well. He had to drive home in a rental car with his side chick. He had to explain to me while he was in the car, and I knew he had the girl with him because the friend told me he didn't go alone. He was giving me a story to cover up his tracks.

I confronted him while he was in New York. He said, "Honey, I'm gonna be late coming home, my flight's delayed."

I said, "Well, you should be home in a few hours then," and it was gonna be seven hours, because he had to drive. When I caught him in his lie, he never admitted having a girlfriend with him, though he did admit going to Paris instead of Florida, where he was initially supposed to go alone. Then I found out it was true from going on her social media page and seeing them celebrate by blowing out a candle on a cupcake on the day before my birthday in Paris.

The Chocolate

Every year, my husband spoiled his staff and others in his profession with gifts and chocolates. I love chocolates. I didn't eat much because I didn't want to gain weight. So, I would crave it at night, and my husband knew this. I would walk around at night, sleepwalk, and find whatever chocolate we had in the house and eat it. I learned about this because I would see the wrappers in the bathroom sink in my own personal bathroom.

During Christmas time, my husband would get several samples of different chocolates to give to his staff and friends. During this period, he would ask me to taste-test the chocolates. Usually, this wasn't a bad idea, but knowing that I had to sample all this chocolate, I knew I would gain weight. And at that time, I had just lost the weight that he had noticed, so I was afraid I might put it back on easily.

I said to my husband, "I love the chocolate. I hope you understand; I enjoy the chocolate. But it's not gonna look good on my waistline. I'm trying to be disciplined."

He got upset with me and told me I didn't appreciate what he did for me, that he would never buy me chocolate again, that his staff deserved it more than I did, and that they were always thankful.

I referred to his staff as his monkeys, who allowed him to behave the way he did toward me. I really didn't care much about what he said. At least I wasn't gonna gain that weight again. I told the story to my friend at the doctor's office, and she felt bad for me. She said he's controlling and has a personality disorder. She said if she could, she would diagnose him herself. And she said he would never hold himself accountable. Accountability was never his strong suit.

I had never heard someone explain that to me about my husband, because she didn't know him. He had never met her. He couldn't show her his charm, his charisma. She wasn't wooed by what he had. She was giving me her honest opinion, no matter how harsh, so I trusted her.

The Empath

I found that I was an empath—someone that feels other people's pain and joy. I found that to be overwhelming at times. I had my own pain that I had to deal with, and I certainly wasn't allowed to experience joy.

As months went by, I kept telling my friend that I trusted what was happening with my husband. She grew worried about my mental health, saying I had given my mental well-being to my husband. I agreed with her. I was falling apart. I no longer felt human. I felt like a robot, something he just used when he needed, mostly for sex.

Material Things

I know I look spoiled with material things on the outside, but on the inside, those material things were hung over my head if I was a bad girl. If he bought me something and I didn't behave properly, he would take it back and tell me that he didn't give it to me, he let me borrow it. As his wife, I didn't understand that. I would post pictures of the gifts he gave me during our marriage on social media, and he would even respond saying, "Happy wife, happy life," or something else very positive. How great of a man on the internet. But at home, he was taking the gifts back.

For example, I received a watch for Christmas, and he took that back after the holidays. I received a silver Louis Vuitton duffel bag for my anniversary, and once he realized that it was a popular bag, he took it back. He told me I didn't deserve the bag, and that it was too expensive for me. I didn't understand his logic: he'd give me a gift he wanted me to have, then take it back. I'd rather he just keep the damn thing and save me the humiliation. I knew what mine was, and I knew what was his. I lived in hell with a smile on my face, to avoid any mental or emotional confusion.

Daily Conversations

In our daily conversations, he would always twist everything I said. He would use it against me, turning regular chats into drama.

I would say to him, "You are weaponizing our conversations all the time."

I enjoy small talk, but I couldn't discuss anything that went on during my day, no matter how small or large. That's something I like to do. He would always think I was trying to gather information to catch him in a lie. I wasn't. I just wanted to know how his day was. I was hoping he would ask me the same, but he didn't. During the time we were having our camp built, we had to hire a local plumber. Under normal circumstances, that would be something rather simple to do, however I was being sexually harassed by the only plumber they have available in town. When I spoke to my husband a few times that the plumber had become 'fresh' with me and asked if he could handle the plumbing up north.

He replied, 'It was my fault that I was being sexually harassed because I never handled it."

I replied, "I did handle it and told my husband. You ignored me each time I complained about this plumber, and now I am uncomfortable being alone with him."

He got mad at me and said, "It is probably because of what you are wearing."

I knew then that I may have loved my husband, but I hated him at the same time.

My husband always told me the same thing whenever I asked about his day. He would say he had a tough day at work and exaggerate a few things at the office. He would complain about a couple of his patients he'd seen that day, and then he'd tell me how much money he had made. After that, he would talk about the problems with his kids, which happened every day. He did this in that order. My husband was very predictable.

Not My House

Just remembering all the times I felt alone in the house—I never could refer to the house as my home. I was told that it wasn't my house; I didn't live there; that I was just a guest while we were married. Shortly after we were married, I returned to my husband's house with two bins of my belongings that I brought from my bedroom like simple things I had on my night stand.

When my husband saw the two bins in the entryway of his house, he asked me, "What is this shit?"

I said, "That shit is my stuff that I brought from my house."

He told me that he had enough shit in his house, and I could put those two bins above the garage. My stuff was all piled up above the garage. It was ridiculous, and it made me feel unwanted.

During our first week of marriage, I felt like a proud wife. I did what I had to do—I went and changed my state driver's license address to his residential address because that's where I would be living now and receiving my mail. After all, that's the law, something one needs to do within 30 days of marriage. I went to the DMV in my state, changed my residence, changed my driver's license, went to his DMV in his state, did the same thing there, and paid what I had to pay.

I waited my three weeks and received my new license. I was so happy and proud of myself, because I had proof that I was his wife, and it seemed like it was my badge of honor—my ID that said my name and address had changed, and I was now his wife. When I showed him my ID after he arrived home from work, to my surprise, he was extremely agitated and pissed.

"Why the fuck did you do that?" he asked in an angry tone.

I couldn't believe it. I almost felt scared at first, and asked, "Why are you getting angry at me for what I'm supposed to do? I explained to him, "Oh, I just changed it because it was law, and I now live here, so I wanted to have that on my ID, and I didn't want to get in trouble."

He told me, "This isn't your fucking house. You don't fucking live here. You have a house in your state. And that's where you're gonna live, and that's what you put on your ID."

"No, I'm gonna live here," I insisted.

"This isn't your house. You're staying here while you're my wife. You have a house in Maine," he replied.

I couldn't believe it. My stomach felt empty, and I really thought I was gonna shit my pants, because I have physical reactions to trauma. I really felt like I was being punished. I agreed with him, then told him I would change my license back to the state of Maine.

"Well, what am I gonna tell them? It's only been three weeks," I asked.

He said, "You tell them that the marriage didn't work out."

And so that's what I did. I went back to the DMV with my license and turned it back into my Maine residence. When I was questioned about it, the clerk asked, "Geez, why are you doing this?"

I said, "Well, the marriage didn't work out."

You could see in her eyes that she felt bad for me—her whole demeanor changed. And honestly, I felt bad for me, too. At least I had someone else who felt pity for me. It reminds me of dogs, who are always loyal to their owners, no matter if they are beaten.

The Ring Cameras

My husband had no idea I got clever with Ring cameras, because he was lying—he was so inconsistent that I couldn't believe anything he said. So, I was questioning, am I imagining this? Am I making shit up? What is happening to me? I needed proof. I wanted physical evidence that I could show someone else besides myself. I didn't even trust myself when I saw it on video, what I was seeing. I had to show someone I trusted, one of my nephews or my son.

I used the Ring Doorbell cameras because you don't need to plug them in, and they alert your phone every time someone walks into the room, and you can hear the conversations. I didn't put the ring cameras in the bathroom or in his living room space, just in my closet, his office, upstairs on the third floor, two rooms where he liked to entertain his female friends that were outside of the marriage, and a camera in my room that I was allowed to hang out in on the first floor, and then a camera in the hallway on the second floor, and a camera under my bed on my side in his bedroom. The bedroom was so big that it didn't expose any privacy of mine, it just showed my side of the bed. It would show who walked into the bedroom.

On the cameras, I heard a conversation when his children were visiting, and they had just left the house. I had a Ring camera by the front door directly under a mirror knowing that they were so vain and would look directly into it, and would never notice the camera.

When they returned about an hour and a half later, his daughter walked in first, and then the father, and then his son came in and said, "Dad, I just don't know why you don't have the fucking whore killed."

He didn't say anything, he just looked at his son, because I can visually see this on the camera on my app.

His daughter said, "Don't worry, I already told Dad she'll be dead soon anyway."

Hearing that and knowing that his son had threatened to kill me earlier, I was really concerned with my well-being. I really was. I sent it to my nephews to see if I should be concerned, and they said yes, because they know that his children are sociopaths, diagnosed during their parents' divorce by doctors. They worried for me, because they had been around my husband when he behaved poorly.

My nephew had witnessed one time when we were playing a game. We had friends over, and we were playing cornhole, which I was doing pretty good. I was on a team with one of my nephews, and my other nephew was playing on the other team with his wife. My husband was watching, and he didn't cheer me on at all, but he was cheering on my nephew's wife. He kept going, "Oh, you're so great, keep doing it, you got this, oh, wow, keep going." He was so obnoxious that my nephew got annoyed and asked me to ask my husband to stop. They both knew not to speak to my husband directly.

So, I simply asked him, "Honey, why aren't you rooting for me? Why do you keep yelling for her and not rooting for me?"

He replied, "Because you suck."

It was evident that he had no love for me. My nephew was disgusted by what he said because I did not do anything to deserve that comment. I was just having fun.

Easter with the Ex-Wife

We weren't allowed to celebrate holidays in the house. I had to celebrate holidays at my house in the state where I was from. I found from one of the cameras that when he had his children over, he celebrated Easter and Thanksgiving with his ex-wife.

When I confronted him about that, I didn't mention the cameras and told him I saw it on social media: his daughter had posted a photo of her and her mother in the foyer. There was a camera there, so I knew they had taken the picture, but I'd never seen it on social media. I don't know what she did with the image. Knowing that, at least I knew if he mentioned it to her, there was some truth to my lie. I had to get just as good at lying as he did to play this game. Because of what I found out about the cameras and how many times he was leaving to cheat on me; I put a tracker on his vehicle. I literally forgot what day it was, what month it was. I was getting exhausted, following my husband on my phone. I was going crazy.

Going Dark

I started getting dark and becoming hateful towards him. Generally, I am a happy-go-lucky person but I was having dark, hateful thoughts about him. While I was losing my mind because I couldn't believe anything he said, I couldn't believe where he said he was going, and I didn't trust anyone around me other than my three nephews and my son. I felt alone. But I wasn't the type of person to just go cry in a room. I did do that occasionally, but eventually, I didn't want to be that person. I didn't want to be a statistic in a toxic relationship.

So, I figured the only thing to keep me sane and together was to get back at him. I started spitting in his food. Every day, when I made his food, I would spit in it. Then, I realized that he had Viagra in his vehicle. He didn't need Viagra in his car, because we never had sex anywhere other than the house. We didn't have an adventurous sex life. I knew that he was using Viagra at the sex spa. I did some homework, and I found that there was a type of laxative pill that looked precisely like Viagra, so I switched out his Viagra for laxatives. If anything, he was gonna shit his pants there, on the way, or on the way home.

The Tea

It got to a point when I did not care about when I fed him. For example, I was supposed to get him his tea every night at 6:30, and I stopped doing that.

He got mad at me and said, "Don't I make your life good enough so you can serve me tea every night?"

"Serve you? I was getting you your tea because I wanted to," I said.

"Well, you're to get my tea every night at 6:30," he said emphatically.

I told him I wasn't going to get him tea unless he asked me to, and he said he'd rather do it himself than ask me for anything. I couldn't believe it.

I repeated what he said to me. "So you would rather do it yourself than simply ask me politely to get it for you?"

"Yes," he replied. So I let him. He started getting his tea himself and complained every night.

Then It Was the Peas

The first time my husband ever called me a cunt was when I forgot to serve him peas at dinner. When he sat down for dinner, he looked at his plate and said, "Where's my peas?"

"Oh, I'm sorry, I forgot them, let me go get them," I replied.

"You're a stupid cunt. You don't have to do anything all fucking day but make sure I have peas on my plate for dinner, and you can't get that right?" he shouted.

I gave him his peas and went and called my sister, crying. I couldn't believe that he had just called me a cunt over peas.

The Doctor Referral

So many times, people would call my husband for a referral to see another person in his profession, or a specific type of doctor. My husband would gladly do this for whoever. He had the personality and the means to get people into doctors' offices either that day or as soon as possible. I've seen him do this hundreds of times.

During our marriage, I became sick with a throat problem that caused me to throw up mucus every morning. I had asked my husband if he could give me a referral to see a doctor to get my throat taken care of, like he had done hundreds of times for other people.

My husband said, "You will need a referral from your doctor. I don't know anyone in that field, in the throat field."

Knowing that I knew that he knew every doctor who worked in at least three states, my feelings were hurt. He wasn't gonna do anything to better my health, and he showed it. Every morning I was coughing up mucus that sat in the back of my throat. It was loud because I was choking on it and it sounded disgusting. My husband would always complain about the noise and how it bothered him to hear me choking on mucus. Yet, he refused to help me.

14

THE BREAKING POINT

The Weight of Control

Trying to keep my weight at 103 pounds at age fifty-one, while aging started to affect my health. I worked so hard to maintain a tiny waist for my husband that I fainted three times in front of him. The first time I passed out, I was upstairs in his bedroom having a simple conversation with him. My knees started tingling, and they buckled. I got dizzy and slowly faded out in front of him. I came to on my own a few minutes later, with my husband still standing there in the same spot where he was when I passed out. I thought, how odd. Did he even try to check on me? Did he try to catch me? Maybe he didn't even see me pass out. How long was I out? These were questions I quickly asked myself. I didn't want to assume he had let me fall and lie there.

The second time I passed out, it was a similar situation. Having a conversation with him when my knees started tingling, I passed out in front of my husband again. This time, I came to and he was still standing there, but this time, he was staring at me. I knew he had seen me pass out, so why didn't he try to help me? When I asked him this, he told me he didn't know what I was talking about.

I said, "I just passed out, and you didn't even try to help me."

"You're overreacting," he replied.

"Okay, but there's something wrong with me. I'm concerned for my health," I said, worried there was something seriously wrong with me.

The third time I passed out in front of my husband, and he didn't help me then either.

I asked him, "Why don't you help me? I passed out three times in front of you, and you just stood there."

He got annoyed with me and told me, "I just don't know what to do with you."

I told him, "What do you mean? It's not me. My knees start tingling, and I pass out." He turned his back towards me and left the room. I was wondering if was passing out because I wasn't eating. If I did eat, he would complain that I was gaining weight. When it came to meals, I was allowed one meal a day, meaning if we were going out for dinner, my husband would remind me that morning that I would not need to eat during the day because we were eating out. He never really saw me eat unless we ate out at a restaurant because at home, I would not eat with him, I would serve him and have to eat after he was done. I usually ate alone in the kitchen.

In a later conversation during the last week of my relationship with him in the house, I was downstairs, and I came upstairs and told him, "I'm not feeling well."

"What's wrong with you?" he asked.

"I think I need to eat something," I replied.

"Well, go eat!" he said. This is when I knew that he was cheating on me because he said that.

"Well, if I eat, I'm gonna put weight on, and you're gonna cheat on me with someone else, and tell me I am fat," I said.

It was at that point that I knew that I didn't want to keep going through that, as I was really struggling to stay at that low weight. That's when I knew he had a girlfriend, because he said, "Go and put on as much weight as you want, honey."

I asked him, "What's her name?"

He looked at me with that same witty smile I saw the entire time during our marriage and said, "Fuck you."

130

Because he had never, ever told me to eat in 22 years. I literally had a doctor tell him, in front of me, that I would look better if I had put on weight.

His reply was, "Oh, that's not gonna happen."

The Lawnmower Incident

A better example of when my husband bought me things but never helped me was when he bought me an expensive lawnmower. Since he never came to the house I owned, I insisted that he get me a simple lawnmower because I knew it would be up to me to put it together and run it. Still, I had to keep up with the lawn and maintain the house because I owned it. He didn't listen to my concerns about getting me the simple lawnmower, and got me the most expensive one he could find.

I had to put the lawnmower together by myself, and that is when I snapped my middle finger between the two handlebars of the mower. When I did that, I scared myself so bad that when I snapped it, it broke my finger. Once I realized I broke my finger, I pulled my finger out of the snapped bar, breaking it a second time.

If he had been there to help me put the mower together like a normal husband would have, I would not have broken my finger. When I was at the hospital and told him what had happened, he hung up on me. He was aggravated by me because I had a problem that really needed attention. I knew better than to bother him with tiny problems so when I reached out, he knew I really needed him, but he had done this before when I had gone off the road during an ice storm, and I was scared. He hung up on me then and only wanted to help me when he wanted to, not when I needed him.

His Ego and the Game

My husband's ego was massive. In fact, once, he compared himself to Tom Brady and Nelson Mandela. When he did this, I laughed at him, which made him angry. He told me he was gonna cheat on me out of spite. He literally said this. He said he'd show me that he was just as good as The Goat. I thought, wow, he is so far up his own ass that I thought he lost his fucking mind. He was gonna cheat on me and let me know that he could get another woman besides myself. At this point in our marriage, I didn't care. I enjoyed getting a chuckle out of his ego. His ego would get bigger after I would confront him about his cheating because he knew I couldn't compete with twenty-year-olds anymore.

I decided then I'd let our marriage play out until the day it didn't any longer. I didn't want to fight for him anymore. It became a game to him to cheat on me, and then I would confront him with it, and then he would like me to fight for him. He literally wanted—his own words—he just liked the fight I had in me for him. And I didn't fight anymore, and he didn't know that. I was faking the smiles. Between the second and third tracker, I found out that my husband was still going to the sex spa.

The Photos

My husband hired a moving company to shift some of our furniture. During the process, the mover had to remove the drawers from one of the dressers to make it easier to lift. While doing so, he pulled out a Ziploc bag containing photos. They seemed to be pictures of a young, nude girl. The mover asked me if I wanted them. I could feel my face turning hot from embarrassment, so I simply told him to put the pictures back in the drawer.

I went downstairs, and because of the look on my face, my husband asked me what was wrong.

I told him, "What had just happened is that there are nude photos in the dresser upstairs in one of the spare rooms.

He simply laughed, and said, "Oh."

I said, "There were photos that looked like a Hispanic girl—naked photos of a young girl that looks like she's Hispanic in the spare room upstairs."

He started to walk out of the room and said, "She's not Hispanic, she's Asian."

I was speechless. He no longer cared about my feelings to even lie about what he was doing.

The Last Confrontation

The last time I followed my husband to the sex spa, I confronted him about it—not revealing that I was tracking him, but I told him I paid a young lady to call me if he ever returned, and she did call me on Friday. She informed me that when my husband arrived, he received full service. "He is always kind to the girls," she said.

Also, he had to return to the spa a second time that day to check on one of the girls—one of the workers who had fallen ill. He prescribed her some medication and wanted to make sure she didn't have an allergic reaction. I confronted my husband with what I knew, and he didn't deny it. In fact, it made him smile, knowing that the young women were speaking positively about him. I finally told my husband that I felt that he was becoming a dirty old man. I had thought it before, but never had the courage to say it to his face. When I did, it was first time I saw shame in his eyes.

Finding My Strength: The Visit to Oakland

After discussing what I knew with my son, I realized there was only one person I could talk to who wouldn't judge me and didn't know my husband. She didn't know anything about his charm, how clever he was with his words, and someone I could be honest with. I flew across the country to visit a friend I hadn't seen in 30 years for her opinion about my situation. I was still doubting myself about what I was going through. I thought I might still love my husband.

After seeking advice from all my friends and hearing only negative comments about myself—saying I deserved it—or that the money was worth the pain and struggle, I reached out to a friend I hadn't seen in a long time. She was someone I could rely on, who always listened and put my feelings first.

Not knowing whether she would have time for me, I went ahead and booked my flight to Oakland, California, anyway. She was so kind! I gave her a quick call and told her what I had done without her permission. To my surprise, she was thrilled to hear about my upcoming visit, but my friend had no idea what was in store for her. When I arrived, my friend wasn't inside waiting for me; she was outside on her steps, as if waiting to see me with anticipation and excitement—something I had never seen or experienced before with any of my friends or husband. My first response was to cry and reach out and hug my friend, Angela. She literally could feel the tension and stress in my body. She hugged me tighter and told me it was gonna be alright, and that she was happy to see me.

During my visit, Angela, her wife, and her son comforted me in a way I had forgotten that a human deserving kindness could. I was allowed to tell my story and be heard. I was allowed to cry and get mad. Finally, I could express myself without judgment. Angela reminded me how strong I was and who I was when I was younger. What I had gone through to get this far in life, but I wasn't going to let a man or anyone else, for that matter, beat me down. I didn't know people could be so nice.

While I was there, I felt stronger both mentally and physically. Angela made sure I ate three meals a day. Her lovely wife would prepare breakfast for me before she went to work, ensuring I got the protein I needed. I couldn't believe this—they were really caring for me. I needed to start my day right, and I couldn't believe there were these people who actually cared about me and wanted nothing from me but my happiness. This was new to me, but I was willing to accept it.

I started to embrace feeling whole again, feeling happy. Angela had reminded me that I could be happy, do things on my own, and needed to live for myself again. I wanted that for myself so badly. When my time had come to an end in Oakland, I knew I would miss her, and I didn't want to fall apart without her being entirely on the other side of the country.

She reassured me with a pat on my ass, "You got this, girl."

I took that energy all the way back home.

The Beginning of the End

Back home, the day came when I decided I was going to leave him. Once I exposed his lies about going to the sex spa in Massachusetts for months, he became much more distant. I knew I had to start my exit. I stopped making his tea, which I used to do every night during our marriage. The dinners I prepared for him were cold because I no longer cared. I stopped greeting him at the door when he left for work, and I stopped taking his calls. I basically stopped being at his beck and call, realizing I was only there to serve him.

A conversation he had had with his son: "Dad, why did you marry the whore?"

"Son, De-De is the only woman who has ever served me the most. She deserves this. She deserves to be my wife." This was a conversation my husband shared with me. His son actually agreed with his father because that's what he was taught—that women were there to serve men.

I called the one friend I still had left who lived near me, who lived at least four hours away. I was never allowed to make friends in the neighborhood, his or mine. I wasn't allowed to make friends with anyone. People would ask too many questions, and I don't naturally lie. I would get in trouble if I told the truth, so it was best that I didn't meet anybody. So, I was kept away from people. He told me that my worst feature is my honesty.

The Final Straw

The night before I left, I tried to load a gun that was on my nightstand. I pictured him without a face because I didn't want to see his face anymore. I put the gun away and decided it was time for me to go. The next morning, I woke up knowing it would upset my husband, so I took some money. I went into his vehicle and took all the money in his console—about $1,000. Later that morning, my husband left for work, and he noticed the money was gone and asked if I took it. I told him yes. He was angry and canceled my credit cards. This didn't surprise me. I knew his behavior was worsening—his feelings for me were getting worse. That day, he came home for lunch, and I told him I wanted to leave.

He said, "I'll have your things packed up this weekend." My husband didn't even ask me why I wanted to leave, and this was Friday.

I told him, "I need a month to move my things myself," and to my surprise, he agreed. That's how simple it was.

"I want to go spend some time at my son's house," I said to him.

"I'll have your things packed," he replied, again without asking me why I wanted to leave. It was clear to me that he didn't care. The burden, meaning me, was walking away, and he was fine with that. He then left for work, and he called me three minutes after, and told me he didn't want a divorce, and that he wanted to fight for me. I laughed and said, "You have never fought for me," and I hung up the phone.

The Prenup and What I Walked Away With

During this time, I tried to find an attorney, which turned out to be rather difficult because everyone knew him and didn't want to take my case. I didn't get an attorney. I told my soon-to-be ex-husband about the difficulties I was facing trying to find an attorney, but he was able to secure one. We had to stick to the prenup which meant I received the bare minimum. I wasn't even asked for my opinion. Yes, he insisted that we have a prenup, so I signed it because I didn't want to be embarrassed. He wasn't planning to marry me unless I signed it. Since my sister was so unpleasant, I didn't want to be embarrassed or made fun of by her if I didn't get married after I got engaged, so I signed the prenup.

Even though he is worth over $20 million, I received $500,000 from the marriage, which was in the prenup.

It didn't matter how long I was going to stay with him. When he died, it was in his will that I was only to get half a million. When I read that, I knew he lied to me because he told me I was going to get a third of his entire inherited assets if I stayed married to him until he died. When I found his will and read it, it stated that I would get what the pre-nup agreement said. I confronted him about it, and he was just aggravated that I read his will and said I was being nosy. He lied to me.

His reason for offering to pack my things was that he wanted to go through them and take back the expensive items he had bought for me. I realized this because while I was packing my own belongings—my nephew and my son helped me—he would watch me pack and ask, "Oh, you're taking that? I bought that."

I would remind him that he bought that for me for my birthday, our anniversary, or Christmas. He called me a pig for taking the things he bought me while we were married. It was insane. By the way, that was his reason for hiring a mover. There was nothing good behind my husband's motives toward me. When he bought me a house—or what I call a camp—it was so he could put me there, have a girlfriend, and build another life with her, knowing I was five hours away.

Reflections: Words on Paper

While I was married, in the last few months, I wrote two poems.

I wanted a husband; he wanted a maid.
I wanted a companion; he wanted a servant.
I wanted a friend; he wanted a slave.
I wanted someone I could lean on; he wanted a soundboard.
I wanted someone I wouldn't be afraid of.
I got a husband.

The second poem I wrote while sitting in the tiny room with windows where I was only allowed to hang out:

I'm just sitting here, all alone,
Sitting in my room of windows.
Looking through the glass,
And all I see is dark.
The day has just begun,
And all I want to do is have fun.
But knowing that I still live here,
I can only think of fear.
You're the last one I count on,
And you're the first one I run from.

I also wrote a letter to my husband, though I never gave it to him:

"Dear Husband of Mine"
You didn't want to have fun with me, so I had to do it alone.
Your lies confused me.
Your insults hurt my feelings.
Your lack of respect made me question my pride.
Your lack of physical touch left me lonely.
Your promises were all empty.
Your jokes were all about me.
Your attention always went to the stranger.
Your anger always went towards me.
You tore me down, tore my confidence down.
And when I worked on myself, I was always the problem.
Your wife.

I felt I could never express anything to him because it was always dismissed as a problem, and I wasn't going to be a problem. If I was going to keep my sanity and pride, I would have to keep everything to myself and use that as a strength to build myself up. I knew deep down that I was working my way out, like digging a small hole each day with a little spoon, knowing that eventually, the hole would get big enough for me to squeeze through.

Each day, I kept taking a verbal beating. He was never physically aggressive; it was always verbal abuse. The silent treatment and never looking at someone—he would respond by not looking at me and saying that I was making it all up. The problem was he never looked at me when he was responding. That drove me nuts.

I would ask him, "Why don't you look at me when I'm talking to you? That's a sign of respect. I know your parents; I know they taught you respect. Why?" It didn't matter.

I hated that, and he loved that. Knowing that I hated something, he would do it more. And if I liked something, it was taken away. So I had to choose what really mattered most to me and keep my own self-respect. He didn't look directly at me for the last year of our marriage when communicating, but he still had sex with me.

Moving Forward

At the age of fifty-two, I made the decision to file for a divorce. Since the ending of our marriage, he's reached out to me a few times. He is now dating one of the young ladies that he met at the sex spa–that is his girlfriend. He had another whole life.

I met him knowing what I was getting into, but I didn't realize how deep it was. I didn't know anything about mental and emotional abuse. I had never even heard of it. I knew about sexual abuse, physical abuse, and abandonment—like when parents leave their kids. But I didn't understand that someone could attack your mind and emotions and take control of them. As a strong person, I was almost fighting that battle with him and myself every day because I thought, "No, he can't beat me at this. I'm smarter than this." But I wasn't. He was smarter than me. I was in a three-ring circus, and I paid for this ticket with my mental health.

I left him in April, and our divorce was finalized in August. I am doing very well. I'm happy. I'm learning how to budget money and financially provide for myself. I grew up poor, so I know how to budget money. I love that I wrote this book. I'm going to do my best to get it out, publish it, and make it meaningful for myself. And I'm investing. I'm doing alright.

I don't believe that I'll ever date again. I've given myself to God, and I'm happy with that. I'm glad I got out. Even though I haven't put on any weight, I don't look so tired and drained, and I have color in my face. I am healthier, feel better, have more energy, and I get to sleep at night. What more could I ask for.

15

NARCISSISM

Understanding Narcissistic Behavior: A Comprehensive Guide

The Nature of Narcissistic Jealousy

A narcissist feels jealous of you from the moment they meet you. At first, they may act like they admire you and put you on a pedestal, seeing you as someone who can make them look good. But over time, their selfish and entitled attitude begins to show. They believe they deserve your success and the good people in your life, so they work to ruin it.

My ex-husband used to say to me, "I don't understand your confidence." He was confused about it and when I would ask him to be more specific, he would say, "Because you were poor growing up, how could you grow up being confident?"

I would say, "I am extremely funny, a loyal companion, and a generous person. I shine in the dark." That pissed him off so bad. He knew my confidence would outshine any negative remark he had for me.

When someone is always jealous of you, they don't want what's best for you—they want to pull you down. That's exactly how a narcissist thinks. They want you to feel small, weak, and dependent on them, whether emotionally or financially. This dependency gives them power, and that's what they truly crave.

They hate to see you happy without them. That's why they often ruin your special moments like birthdays, celebrations, or achievements. They'll dismiss your awards as insignificant or claim your success doesn't matter. Narcissists do this to feel better about themselves.

I took private pilot flying lessons, and he paid $30,000 for my lessons, but he did not show up for my test. Knowing he never supported me in my accomplishments, no matter how big or small, I told him I passed my test so he wouldn't be disappointed in me. I failed because I could not land the plane. I lied to save myself from humiliation at his hands. Narcissists can't tolerate seeing others do better than them, so they'll try to drag you down, so that is why I lied to him.

Do Narcissists Fake All Relationships?

Not at first, but that doesn't mean the relationship won't become fake over time. Narcissists can fall for romantic partners just like anyone else. The problem is they can't let the relationship grow and develop healthily because they're self-centered and only care about themselves. In the beginning, narcissists often put their partner on a pedestal. But no one can live up to that unrealistic image. Eventually, they start to devalue you, even though they still want to keep the relationship going.

At the beginning of knowing my ex-husband, he surprised me at least twice a week with gifts, vacations, and flattered me with compliments. Once I became his official girlfriend, it was like a switch had been turned on. I asked him, coming home from a vacation, "What is wrong with you?"

"What do you mean?" he asked.

"You have become really angry all the time," I replied.

"This is the real me," he said. "Get used to it."

He treated me better when he paid for my company.

They have many reasons for maintaining this now "fake" relationship:
- You might be very loving, and they see you as a replacement for the mother figure they never had
- You might act like their loyal assistant, waking them up, reminding them of appointments, or taking care of their needs
- You might have money, resources, or assets they don't want to lose
- You might fulfill their sexual desires and do whatever they want in bed

Whatever the reason, narcissists are capable of faking love and devotion for years—as long as it benefits them. But they don't love you; they love what you provide for them. Meanwhile, they'll often have other fake relationships on the side. Some might be friends who listen to their stories, others might feed their ego by admiring them, and some might just be used for sex. Anyone my husband is around only there because they stroke his ego. He will not go anywhere without getting praise. I would say to him, "You have everyone at the end of your dick." I had no one on my side.

Five Common Addictions Narcissists Often Have

Narcissists are often seen as confident, charming, and in control. But behind this mask, many of them are deeply insecure. They hide their pain and fear by pretending to be stronger, smarter, and more powerful than they really are. To keep up this act, they often turn to different types of addictions. These addictions help them feel better in the moment, but they also hurt others and create tremendous damage over time.

1. Sex Addiction: Craving Attention and Power

Narcissists often use sex as a way to feel powerful, loved, and important. For them, sex is not always about closeness or love. Instead, it becomes a tool to get attention or to feel in control. They may have many partners or cheat on their spouse. They might lie, manipulate, or flatter someone just to get them into bed.

This behavior is not really about pleasure. It's more about filling a deep emptiness inside. Narcissists want to feel desired, needed, and admired. The moment someone gives them attention; they feel a rush. But this feeling doesn't last long, so they look for the next person to provide them with that same high.

This kind of addiction hurts both the narcissist and the people involved. It destroys trust, damages relationships, and can lead to a life of lies, guilt, and loneliness. Narcissists may act like they don't care, but deep down, they are often scared of being alone or unwanted.

2. Stealing: Feeling Entitled to Take

Narcissists often believe they deserve special treatment. They think they are more important than others and should get whatever they want. Because of this, they might steal—not just money or things, but also ideas, credit for others' work, or even someone else's partner.

Sometimes, stealing gives the narcissist a feeling of power. They enjoy taking from others because it makes them feel smart, sneaky, or in control. Other times, they steal because they are jealous or want to punish someone they feel has more than them. They rarely feel guilty about stealing. In their minds, they are just taking what they believe they deserve. If they do get caught, they may lie or blame someone else. This makes it hard for others to trust them. Over time, this addiction can destroy jobs, friendships, and family ties. It shows how little the narcissist respects others and how far they will go to feed their own needs.

No matter how weird he acted, he never stole anything, but he would take credit for any great idea I had. For example, I decorated for Halloween every year, and when people would come over to admire the decorations, he would tell them, "It took me all week long." But he didn't lift a finger, just dictated where he wanted the decorations, especially the moving Halloween characters like witches or ghosts. They are called Animatronics.

3. Chaos Addiction: Creating Drama and Confusion

Many narcissists are addicted to chaos. They can't stand peace or quiet because it forces them to face their own emptiness. So instead, they create drama, start fights, or stir up trouble. This keeps everyone's attention on them and distracts them from their own inner pain. They may:

- Start arguments over small things
- Play people against each other
- Change stories or lie to confuse others
- Blow problems out of proportion

Chaos gives them a sense of control. If everyone is stressed or confused, the narcissist feels like the one in charge. They feed off others' emotional energy, especially when those emotions are fear, anger, or sadness.

But living in constant chaos is exhausting—for both the narcissist and those around them. It damages mental health, ruins relationships, and often leads to broken homes and toxic work environments. Still, the narcissist may not stop unless they lose something big or someone finally walks away.

I told my ex-husband that it is exhausting to be around him. I had no idea if he was going to explode or lash out at me for something that happened at work that was not that big a deal. He would exaggerate every little thing so he could get angry with me.

I told him, "Don't take it out on me. You are angry at the wrong person." He wasn't really angry at all, he just wanted to ruin my day.

4. Gossip Addiction: Tearing Others Down to Lift Themselves Up

Narcissists often use gossip as a weapon. They talk badly about others to make themselves look better. If someone else is doing well or getting attention, the narcissist may spread lies or secrets to bring them down. They enjoy watching others fall, especially if it makes them feel more powerful or important.

This kind of behavior is very harmful. Gossip can destroy reputations, friendships, and families. But to the narcissist, it feels like a win. They get to control how others see the person they gossip about, and they often enjoy the reaction it causes. Narcissists may say things like:

- "I probably shouldn't tell you this, but…"
- "Did you hear what she did?"
- "I just want to help, but I'm worried about them."

They pretend to care while actually trying to damage someone else's image. This addiction to gossip keeps them feeling powerful and in control of social situations.

People around them often walk on eggshells, afraid of becoming the next target. This creates a toxic and fearful environment.

5. Control Addiction: Needing to Be in Charge of Everything

At the heart of all these behaviors is a deep need for control. Narcissists fear being powerless, ignored, or exposed. To avoid these feelings, they try to control everything and everyone around them. This need becomes an addiction. They may control through:

- Emotional manipulation
- Gaslighting (making others question their reality)
- Giving silent treatments
- Setting rules no one else agreed to
- Withholding love, support, or resources

In relationships, this kind of control can be especially damaging. It leaves others feeling confused, small, and dependent. The narcissist may act kind one moment and cruel the next, keeping others off-balance so they never feel safe or sure of themselves. The more control the narcissist has, the more powerful they feel. But it's never enough. They always want more, and they panic when they feel it slipping away. This addiction can lead to abuse, isolation, and long-term emotional damage to those around them.

My ex-husband was really good at holding money over me because he was in charge of our finances. If I ever needed money for anything important, he made sure my behavior was tip-top that day so I could receive it. I didn't just want it, I needed it. Once he recognized that need, he held it over me.

Why Narcissists Get Addicted

All these addictions have one thing in common: they help the narcissist avoid facing their true self. Underneath their confidence and charm, many narcissists feel empty, unworthy, or ashamed. These feelings are too painful for them to handle, so they create a false version of themselves—a version that appears strong, successful, and in control.

But keeping up this false image takes a lot of energy. The narcissist becomes desperate for ways to keep the mask from slipping. That's where their addictions come in. Each addiction gives them a quick fix:
- Sex makes them feel desired
- Stealing makes them feel clever and powerful
- Chaos keeps attention on them
- Gossip boosts their ego
- Control keeps their fear of weakness away

Unfortunately, these fixes never last. The emptiness always returns, and the cycle begins again. The more they feed their addictions, the more damage they cause—to themselves and to others. That is why I stayed. I knew him like no one else, and I knew he was suffering, and I felt bad for him as a human, but I became his punching bag. You may notice that I said several times throughout this book that I felt bad for him. If he could be himself once, he would be so happy. He was jealous that I could be who I was. He could not.

The Cost of Narcissistic Addictions

The people closest to narcissists often suffer the most. They may feel confused, hurt, and trapped. It's hard to understand why someone would lie, cheat, steal, or create chaos on purpose. Victims of narcissists may blame themselves, thinking they caused the bad behavior. But the truth is, the narcissist's addictions have nothing to do with love or care. They are about control, power, and covering up inner wounds. Over time, these behaviors can lead to:

- Divorce or broken relationships
- Lost jobs or career problems
- Financial troubles
- Legal issues
- Health problems (mental and physical)
- Loneliness and isolation

And even though narcissists may seem like they're winning—getting what they want, staying in control—they often end up alone, angry, and still empty inside. My ex-husband hides behind his money.

The Three-Step Cycle of Narcissistic Abuse

Narcissists have three main ways they mess up your life if you let them:

1. Ignore Your Feelings

Whenever you tell a narcissist how you feel, they don't care and show they don't care. Over time, this can make you doubt your self-worth.

A couple of years into our relationship, he kept trying to be clever with his insults to me.

One day, I asked him, "Can you not say that to me? You hurt my feelings."

His response was, "Can you tell me when I hurt your feelings? Because it upsets me and I don't want to ruin my day."

I said, "Did you just hear what you said? You asked me not to tell you when you upset me. Try not to be an asshole."

I couldn't believe it.

2. Undermine Your Thoughts

Whenever you tell a narcissist what you want to do, they say things like "Are you sure?" "That's crazy," or "You'd be happier if you did what I want." This constant undermining makes you doubt your own judgment and become dependent on the narcissist's advice.

Every time I told my husband what I was planning for myself to do, like a trip or even something simple as lunch, his first comment was always negative, like it may or may not happen, putting fear into my mind and making me doubt myself. So, I would often never leave my little room that he provided for me. I became a hermit.

3. Bully Your Actions

If ignoring your feelings and undermining your thoughts doesn't get you to do what the narcissist wants, they will threaten you, yell at you, criticize you, or humiliate you. This constant bullying makes you lose confidence in standing up to the narcissist.

If you experience this three-step cycle, you may feel tired and deflated. But trying to share these feelings with the narcissist will just start the cycle all over again—they don't care about your emotional needs, only their own. As long as you are trapped in this cycle, it will damage your self-worth, self-autonomy, and self-confidence. Your top priority should be to escape this cycle, especially if you are still a child dependent on the narcissist. Breaking free is crucial for your psychological health.

During my relationship with my husband, my brother, mother, uncle and two of my friends died, and not one time did he console me. His response was, "I don't even know them. "I never got to mourn any of them in a healthy way. I cried in my closet alone and once I knew he needed something, I freshened up and went downstairs and acted like everything was normal. I didn't even get flowers when my mother died from my husband.

The Narcissist's Core Problem

The narcissist's problem is everything—including themselves, their issues, and even their unresolved childhood problems. They're miserable people, but they'll never admit it. The narcissist never realizes that they're the common link to all the problems in every relationship they're in. One of their most significant issues is that they hate being wrong—even when they know they are. For example, if a narcissist robbed a bank and got caught, they'd still come up with some excuse to justify why they didn't do it. Even with clear video evidence showing their face, they'd still deny it or twist the story to make themselves look innocent.

Nothing you do for them is ever good enough. They're takers, not givers. If they do something for you, there's always a price or a condition attached. They put no effort into relationships and don't care why they aren't growing or improving. Narcissists have a severe thinking disorder and major personality issues. They never see themselves as the problem, even though they know the difference between right and wrong. What's scariest is that they even believe their own lies.

Narcissists are too cowardly to physically harm you directly, but they'll slowly destroy you over time with their cycle of emotional abuse. Anyone who escapes a relationship with a narcissist with their life and sanity intact is fortunate. Unless a narcissist finds someone new who can give them more than you do, they'll likely stay with you. But remember, it's not real love; it's all about what they can get from you.

That is why he married me. He told his son that I was the one who served him the most.

Why Narcissists Do Not Love Their Children

1. Their Love Is Conditional

One primary trait in the relationship between a narcissistic parent and their children is how their love is conditional. A parent is supposed to show unconditional love to their children. It doesn't mean they should enable everything, but it does mean accepting the child for who they are. However, a narcissistic parent's love is transactional—like a deal.

You only get their love when you meet their expectations and make them look good. If you don't, you get devalued and sometimes even tossed aside. Love and attention are only given when the child does what the parent wants; it's all about the child meeting the parent's expectations.

2. They Love Control and Compliance

When kids grow up between ages 3 and 15, they're less likely to question authority. This is when the narcissistic parent finds it easy to shape you, to mold you into their image. It can look like fondness, but it's more about control and making you obey. They choose what you study, they pick the school you go to, and they even choose your friends.

You don't get to have your own identity; you become just an extension of them. If you try to show your individuality, your differences, your uniqueness, suddenly you're seen as trouble, and then the alarm goes off in their head, and the attack starts. In my case, my husband did not like his children at all. He had them to please his second wife and made no effort into raising them at all. He hired four nannies to do the job, who unfortunately, allowed them to do whatever they wanted to do, good or bad, causing them to grow up into bad adults.

3. They Show Affection for Public Approval

Narcissistic parents lavish affection on their kids in public, but really, it's all about getting attention and admiration from others. When they're alone with their children, they can be cold and disconnected, like they don't care. But as soon as they're out in public and people are watching, suddenly they're the nicest, sweetest, best parents ever.

This creates a confusing dynamic. Did the child do something amazing to deserve this sudden affection? Is the parent happy with them for some reason they don't even know? That's exactly how it feels to have a narcissistic parent with this Dr. Jekyll and Mr. Hyde personality, and this is where the trauma bond begins. Beneath it all, the parent's primary goal isn't really about the child's happiness or well-being; it's all about the show.

Things Narcissists Never Do

1. They Never Give Compliments

One of the first things you'll notice about narcissists is that they rarely give compliments. If it seems like they did, look closely—you'll often find that the compliment was given to benefit them in some way. They don't give sincere compliments because they don't want other people to feel good about themselves. Instead, they withhold genuine praise and will often brag about themselves. Their goal is to keep the spotlight on them, not you. I figured this out long ago–he always had a motive for any compliment.

2. They Won't Ever Apologize

Even if you catch them red-handed with clear proof they did something wrong, they will still refuse to say sorry. Why? Because apologizing means taking responsibility, and narcissists will avoid accountability at all costs. In fact, instead of apologizing, they'll often twist the situation around and blame you for what they did. This is one of their most confusing tactics because most people think, "I would never do that, so surely they wouldn't either." That's how many people end up believing the narcissist's false version of reality. Something as simple as breaking a candle in Wal-Mart, my husband caused a huge scene, blaming me for doing it, but it flipped out of his hand. It was a simple mistake, but he would not take responsibility for it. Embarrassed, I left him in the aisle.

3. They Will Never Give Up Control

Control is everything to a narcissist. They want to make you believe you can't do anything without them. If you try to prove them wrong, they will try to make you fail. This is why divorcing a narcissist or dealing with custody battles can drag on for years. They don't care about the damage it causes you—or even their own children. In fact, some narcissists go so far as to create lies or even fake evidence just to paint you as the problem. Their goal is always the same: to keep control and make their version of reality win.

4. Helping Someone Anonymously

You'll also never see a narcissist do something good in secret. If they donate money, help someone, or do a kind act, they'll want recognition for it. They don't do good deeds just to help others; they do them to polish their image and make themselves look good in public. That way, if anyone tries to expose their abusive behavior, people might not believe it because "how could such a generous person do something so awful?"

At the heart of it, everything a narcissist does is for themselves. They don't see others as equals. They need to feel like they are the most important, the most successful, and the most admired person in the room. You won't see them surround themselves with people who are more successful, wealthier, smarter, or better-looking because being around someone "superior" makes them feel small and jealous.

For a narcissist, nothing is worse than being outshone. Their whole life is built around avoiding that feeling, even if it means tearing others down to feel on top, or their spouse for that matter.

The Narcissistic Collapse

At some point, a narcissist goes through something called a "narcissistic collapse," usually as they get older. People stop putting up with their behavior, and they end up alone with their own thoughts.

Narcissists get their energy from other people. They need others to feel important and in control. You could say they're like emotional parasites—they depend on people to feel powerful. But when everyone finally walks away, they have no one left to use. That's when all the pain and problems they've been hiding come out, and they fall into a deep depression. They shut down and isolate themselves.

This kind of depression is much worse than what most people feel because narcissists don't have a real sense of self-worth. Inside, they feel empty and hopeless. That's why you don't need to get revenge on a narcissist. Life eventually catches up with them. Sometimes they realize something's wrong, but most of the time they just keep sinking, feeling more rejected, more depressed, and more alone.

In the end, everyone leaves a narcissist. People can only take the abuse and manipulation for so long—then they finally wake up and walk away for good.

Strange Messaging Habits of Narcissists

For narcissists, texting isn't just texting. It's not like texting a friend, colleague, or family member who respects your time and has clear boundaries. It feels like you are stepping into a psychological mind game, and everything—from the punctuation to the response time—is weaponized against you.

What should have been a normal exchange of messages becomes a mechanism of punishment, manipulation, and control. They don't simply reach out to see how you're doing; they are messaging to test your loyalty, jumpstart anxiety, and demand you put them center stage in your life.

If you have ever felt emotionally drained, baffled, or guilty after what should have been a casual back-and-forth, you were likely subjected to these bizarre texting habits. From demanding quick replies to texting you at the worst possible times to taking your words out of context and literally accusing you of monstrous behavior, narcissists can wreak havoc on communication as we know it.

And yet, the bizarre nature of this behavior and the discomforting feeling we are left with are often so peculiar that most people who have not experienced it would simply not believe it exists. I lived that every day. Communication with my husband was all about control, manipulation, and gaslighting. It was exhausting for me just to ask him how his day went. In my mind as a wife, I thought that if I put in the time and effort to give him what he needed for communication, that I would receive some sort of gentleness, but it was always surrounded with confusion and madness.

How Narcissists Handle Breakups

Narcissists are disordered individuals; they are fundamentally different from healthy people. Narcissists don't form genuine emotional attachments. When someone leaves a narcissist, they suffer because they've lost a source of supply. Their egos are damaged, and they often feel insulted. Narcissists take it personally when someone leaves them. They will try to hoover you to pull you back into the relationship; if they fail, they will look for other options. Once a narcissist finds alternatives, they feel better. Leaving narcissists will only cause them narcissistic injury.

If narcissists leave someone, then they don't care because they have already moved on much before the relationship ends. Narcissists don't have problems getting over relationships as long as they keep finding options. They don't miss the person; they only miss the narcissistic supply they were getting from the person. Narcissists don't love anyone, so they don't experience pain after a breakup like healthy people do.

I believe that is why my husband continued going to the sex shop, so he could have a constant supply of what he craved, and that was control and physical touch.

Is Monkey Branching a Sign of Narcissism?

Narcissists are notorious for "monkey branching"—while they may not have invented the concept, they certainly excel at it. In this dynamic, a narcissist often has a new partner lined up before they end things with their current one. This allows them to seamlessly transition from one relationship to another, as the new partner is already making adjustments to meet the narcissist's demands. The goal is to ensure everything is in place for when the narcissist decides to discard their current partner, allowing for an effortless leap into the next situation.

Female narcissists frequently employ monkey branching, often seeking to drain their current partner's resources to alleviate their own financial burdens. They may aim to leave their partner in a precarious financial and emotional position before moving on. This behavior, which can be seen as a form of cheating, demonstrates a profound lack of respect. Narcissists engage in this without a hint of guilt or remorse, mirroring their approach to infidelity.

What Narcissists Actually Love

Indeed, they do love. In the end, they are somewhat human; they have feelings and emotions. From among the things that those creatures love—and it's certainly not you: they truly love themselves more than anything else. They love to feed on your emotions. They love drama; they love to lie; they love hate; they love manipulation; they love malice; they love to hurt; they love hidden facades.

They take pleasure in seeing you broken, and they definitely love seeing you in pain. You have to know something about narcissists: they hate to see you strong, healing, and coping. They had that injury from childhood that they never coped with. It is what makes them bitter, vengeful, and full of hate, and they will love to hoover you back just to destroy the rest of you.

They love escaping anything after being discarded as if nothing happened. They love to play innocent, they love to look good, and they always love to be right.

Dog Whistling

One of the narcissistic games they play nearly every time is known as dog whistling. Dog whistling occurs when a narcissist makes some comment publicly or in a public area that is innocent (or even complimentary) to everyone else involved, but you catch the ulterior motive. It's similar to an actual dog whistle only you can "hear" it, because you're aware that there's something going on behind the scenes. For instance:

Suppose your narcissistic partner has just recently been yelling at you in the house for having it not clean enough. Then, you and the narcissist go to a dinner party at Susan and John's.

Suddenly, the narcissist will remark, "Wow, Susan, I'm so impressed that your house is so clean. You're such a good mom!"

To the group, it is a pleasant compliment. But to you, it is a backhanded compliment intended to shame and humiliate you. You understand that they are making an implicit comparison of you with Susan, pointing out your real or imagined flaws to everyone.

Now you're gasping for breath as Susan and John are thinking, "What's she crying about something positive for?" To the world outside, you're too sensitive, maybe even crazy. Meanwhile, the narcissist has achieved exactly what they desired: destroying you and still maintaining their façade.

That's the devious part of dog whistling: hidden abuse in disguise as harmless conversation, and you're left feeling alone, not believed, and confused. My husband did this every time we went out anywhere or with anyone. He would say that he feared for his life living with me. I told him, "One of these days, someone is going to believe you."

He said, "Good. I hope they do."

It was constant.

The Game of Mind Tricks

The narcissistic game of mind tricks is not done until they play the final card, which isn't a trick at all but rather a performance to screw with you emotionally and mentally, forcing you to question every last bit of yourself.

Picture this: After the manipulation and all of the emotional ups and downs, just when you thought you were done, they pull a stunt that takes you for yet another ride. This isn't ghosting; it's a disappearing act that simultaneously strips you of your self-esteem and confidence. They concoct such a believable story that even those closest to you can't take your side. It's psychological warfare, and you're left trying to piece your mind back together without even knowing what just happened.

This card is the narcissist's ultimate method of bringing attention back to themselves. They will twist the story so they become the victim or the hero, and the true victim of the narcissist's abuse is now the bad guy in everyone else's eyes. It is as if every account of your side of the story has been erased, and your suffering has been erased from the story of your life.

But there's a catch—it will not just be a play; it will be your chance to be free. If they are playing their last card, then it is also their admission of defeat. They have played their final card. Your freedom is now assured. Now you can begin to rebuild your life and your own story.

The time has come for you to rise up and seize what they have left behind and build something powerful, stable, and authentic to you. This is your time to shine and build a life they can never breach.

When the narcissist plays the last trick, just smile. Know that the opportunity to begin the next chapter is where you have won. You have taken everything they purportedly took from you and transformed it into strength and wisdom. Now you are in control. Your foundation is as solid as a rock. You have grown tall, and the game is up. You have won.

You, too, can also break away from the generational trauma as I did myself. I hope that reading this book will inspire you to do the same.

*A narcissist can swiftly
enter another relationship
because when shallow connections
are all they can manage,
deep healing remains unnecessary.*

A NOTE TO THE READER

If this book stirred difficult emotions, memories, or experiences for you, or if you recognize your own story, or the story of someone you love, please know that you are not alone, and help is available. Emotional, psychological, and physical abuse can have lasting effects, but healing is possible with the right support. Reaching out for professional help is a sign of strength, not weakness.

If you or someone you know is experiencing domestic violence or abuse, please contact the National Domestic Violence Hotline at 1-800-799-7233 or visit thehotline.org. For mental health emergencies, call 988 (Suicide & Crisis Lifeline).

If this book resonated with you, a review on the retailer where you purchased it is deeply appreciated. Your review helps amplify this story and may encourage others who need it to find their way toward healing and hope.

You deserve safety, care, and the opportunity to heal.

Much love,
De-De

ABOUT THE AUTHOR

De-De is a first-time author whose work explores resilience, identity, and the long path from trauma to self-reclamation. Raised in a deeply unstable environment marked by poverty, neglect, and abuse, she learned early how survival often requires silence, endurance, and adaptation. These formative experiences shaped both her struggles and her strength, setting the stage for a life defined by perseverance rather than defeat.

As a young adult, De-De sought structure and belonging through basic training in the military service, later navigating years of instability, addiction, and destructive relationships while striving to build a sense of safety and self-worth. Motherhood became a turning point, anchoring her determination to break generational cycles of abuse and create a healthier life for herself and her son. Her journey includes confronting mental health challenges, recognizing patterns of emotional and psychological harm, and ultimately choosing boundaries, self-respect, and healing.

Now in her early fifties, De-De considers herself a true survivor. Someone who has learned to trust her instincts, honor her resilience, and rebuild from the inside out. *The Ring That Changed Nothing* is her unflinching account of childhood trauma, toxic marriage, and the hard-won rediscovery of self. Through her writing, she hopes to offer recognition, validation, and courage to others who are learning that survival can become strength.